Shadows of the Shoah

Shadows of the Shoah
Jewish Identity and Belonging

Victor Jeleniewski Seidler

Oxford • New York

First published in 2000 by
Berg
Editorial offices:
150 Cowley Road, Oxford, OX4 1JJ, UK
838 Broadway, Third Floor, New York, NY 10003-4812, USA

Berg is an imprint of Oxford International Publishers Ltd.

Library of Congress Cataloging-in-Publication Data
A catalogue record for this book is available from the Library of Congress.

British Library Cataloguing-in-Publication Data
A catalogue record for this book is available from the British Library.

ISBN 1 85973 355 7 (Cloth)
      1 85973 360 3 (Paper)

Typeset by JS Typesetting, Wellingborough, Northants.
Printed in the United Kingdom by WBC Book Manufacturers, Mid Glamorgan.

Contents

In memory of all those who perished in the Ickowitz, Jeleniewski, Placek and Seidler families during the Shoah – and for the third generation:

Daniel and Lily
Paulo and Juliana
Philippa, Beverley and Louise,
Eyal, Ilana and Ben.

And do as our hold Sages have done – pour forth your words and cast them into letters. This will be the greatest retribution which you can wreak upon these wicked ones. Despite the raging wrath of our foes the holy souls of your brothers and sisters will then remain alive. These evil ones schemed to blot out their names from the face of the earth; but a man cannot destroy letters. For words have wings; they mount up to the heavenly height and they endure for eternity.

[Rabbi Nachum Yanchiker – the last Musar talk delivered in the Slabodka Musar-Yeshiva, Kovno, moments before the German invasion. *Days of Awe* (Reform Synagogues of Great Britain, London, 1985, pp. 497–8)]

Preface

I was in Warsaw station, waiting with the luggage, as Anna went off to report that her wallet had been stolen on the train from Krakow. A small and well-organized gang had blocked the entrance to the carriage as we got on in Krakow and were pushing against us as they attempted to rob us. I should have realized what was happening but it was only as I got into the carriage that I said to Anna that I thought someone had tried to pickpocket me. Waiting in the station for Anna felt fine at the beginning but then I felt very uneasy and nervous. I knew that she was not far but somehow I could not help feeling that she had been kidnapped and I would not see her again. I became all hot and felt a throbbing pain. I tried to still myself but I could not really do it. I thought up to then that I had been handling our trip to Poland reasonably well. We had chosen not to visit Auschwitz or Treblinka this time and the trip, though very difficult and emotional at times, had made us feel close and connected, as we shared our individual histories in Poland.

Now I felt tense and when Anna returned from a different direction about forty minutes later I knew that I just needed to leave. I could not deal with the insecurities that were emerging and I felt terribly unsafe. I felt that I just wanted to leave Warsaw as fast as I could for I felt strangely threatened. I had had enough and just wanted to be safely waiting for the aeroplane at the airport. I did not expect to feel this way. Anna gave me a Bach flower remedy that she always has at hand. But it did not really do the trick. I felt scared. My family had not been able to leave Warsaw alive and they had all perished in the war. My father had been lucky to be in England when the war broke out. He was never to see his family again and was only slowly to hear the news about them. He was not to hear their voices again.

For years as I grew up in England I wanted to be 'like everyone else'. I learned to think that I had had a happy childhood, even though my father died when I was just five in 1951. I wanted to believe that my family was 'normal' and that we were like any other English family, though of course they were not. But it was difficult for me to feel otherwise. Somehow I felt that I owed it to my mother to be 'normal' and so it was difficult to register my history and the ways that I carried the voices of my mother and father and the families which they lost in the war. I did not heed these voices because for years it felt too threatening to listen.

I had been invited to visit Poland for the second time. I had not really thought much about it, though for much of the year it was on the horizon of my consciousness. Anna had decided that she wanted to come with, though it was not going to be easy to organize care for our children, Daniel and Lily. She had never really spoken about wanting to go to Poland before. She was clear that she did not want to visit any of the camps but she did want to visit the towns her parents had come from. It felt important for us to go together and we organized that we would go and return together, even if it meant that we would only have a few days there. But this was part of an emotional journey that, in our individual ways, we had been on for years. At some level it was tied up with our relationship with each other and some of the difficulties that we had had to work through. Anna was the daughter of survivors and I was the son of refugees. We were both children of the post-Shoah Jewish diasporas. Both our families had been displaced and were no longer growing up where they had once expected to grow up. My father had come from Poland and both of Anna's parents had originally come from there. In our relationship, lost elements of the diaspora were coming together.

We had different experiences of the diaspora. I was closely identified with England where I was born. Anna was born in Regensberg in Southern Germany after her parents had been released from camps, before they went on to New York for seven years. Eventually they decided to move to Sao Paulo, Brazil. Anna thinks of herself as Brazilian and strongly identifies with the Brazilian history, culture, language as well as music, although we have lived together in London for over twenty years. Our experience is not centred in one place; rather we live between different places. This is part of the experience of living in the diaspora, but neither of us thought of ourselves as 'Polish'. This particular cord had been severed and Anna had been constantly told in her family that 'the Poles were worse than the Germans'. It was not easy to know, as a child, what to make of this, but it was said so often that it registered on different levels.

As the trip came closer we both became anxious in our own ways. Anna was wondering whether she could go through with it and whether she really wanted to go. Some of our anxieties were focused upon the cold and on reports of how bad the weather might be. I wanted to finish some writing and so distracted myself in this way. At the same time I wanted everything to be organized, which it was not. I kept putting things off and we only made final arrangements very late. It was a journey that we wanted to take, but it was also a journey that we feared. We each had to come to terms with it in our own way. We knew this would not be easy and that we had to learn to give space to each other as well as love and support. I want to share my experiences of the journey, knowing that Anna will work this out in her own way.

As soon as I returned from Poland I felt a need to write out some of what had happened. Somehow the trip allowed me to feel different and it seemed, as least for a moment, to lift a particular kind of pressure. I understood a little more of where I had come from and what the family had gone through. I felt a little easier, despite all the pain and destruction. Somehow I did not feel that I had to be 'like others', for I could recognize more readily that I had my own particular history. I had somehow gained an experience that stretched back through the Holocaust. It was no longer the vast black hole – the full stop it had been for so long. But this helped me think about my identity, both personally and theoretically, in different ways, about diasporas and belonging. For years, especially as a child, I felt that I should feel like others and if I did not there must be something wrong with me. I should either pretend that I do and if I do this hard enough, I will begin too. I should learn to hide whatever differences I feel, for otherwise I would be rejected. At some level this is tied in with a particular conception of Jewish masculinities and the unspoken fears of the 'feminization' of Jewish masculinities that have been so central to fascist ideologies.

This writing, which is both personal and theoretical, raises questions that I have been trying to express for a while. It is the beginning of an exploration, a first step in a continuing process. Although sharing a particular journey and reflecting upon a particular experience of Jewish identity I hopefully will reflect upon more general themes of identity, memory and belonging. The Jewish experience of diasporas has been taken as some kind of example for reflections on other diasporic experiences. Refusing the assimilationist demand to centre experience and loyalties in a single space, there is a growing recognition of how people can live between different spaces. Sometimes these are spaces, like Poland, about which we can remain quite unconscious. It is only through visiting that we learn how 'Jewish' is tied up with 'Polish', even though we might have learned these as antagonistic terms, and the Jews and the Poles in Poland very much lived as separate communities. The ties operated at different levels. They had to do with food, but also with attitudes and relationships. They had to do with forms of life.

I want to thank Daniel and Lily who supported us in making the journey in so many different ways. I want to thank Anna and Simon for being there as a crucial support. In the weeks before the trip as I found myself linked to the sense of loss and destruction, I cried for those whose individual loss I could begin to feel at the memorial service held on the first day of Succoth, the Jewish festival. I appreciated the support after the service offered by Rabbi Marcia Plumb who also kindly sent us the New York times article on 'Poland's New Jewish Question' by Ian Buruma. She thought it would be helpful to prepare us for the trip and it was. My men's group at Spectrum also heard me out on the evening before the flight. I shared a dream and some of the feelings that had been gathering over the last few weeks. They listened and that was what I needed.

My mother shared some of her experience on our regular Friday shopping expeditions. We sat in the coffee house and she said what she could. She also acknowledged what she did not know, which was important too. My brother Tony shared his reflections and his photographs of a much longer trip to Poland that he had made with two friends the year before. He helped us prepare for what we could expect and, as always, was generous with his time and attention. Gail, Philippa. Beverley and Louise were also supportive and it was lovely to see them at the book launch for *Man Enough* we had in the week before the trip. I shared some of my fears and excitement with the many friends who were there. I am sure it was their support and love which carried us through. It was a source of strength that we could draw upon whenever we needed on the journey and also later when we returned.

I felt an urgency to write out some of this history, which can still feel so precarious to me. I wanted to be able to share it with the next generation, so that possibly they will not feel so silently burdened by not knowing as we often were, being a second generation. But in writing for my own extended family, those who survived and have been able to grow up in relative security, I am also writing for other families who might know even less.

Introduction

Making Visible: Identities and Anxieties

James Shapiro has recently published *Shakespeare and the Jews,* which is a book not so much about Shakespeare as it is about the culture of which he was a part.[1]

A professor of English and comparative literature at Columbia, he argues that scholars have overlooked the role that Jews played in helping the English define themselves. Events in the sixteenth and seventeenth centuries worked to complicate stable notions of English identity. The Reformation had pitted Catholics against Protestants and the quest for empire was reshaping nations. In an interview for *The Chronicle of Higher Education,* 2 February 1996, Shapiro says that 'At a time when many writers were trying to reinvent what it meant to be English, the English increasingly defined themselves by whom they were not. Very often that was the Jews. I would argue that the English were obsessed with the Jews' (p. 8).

Like many post-Holocaust Jewish scholars, James Shapiro had kept his Jewish identity separate from his professional work. Although he was raised in a traditional, observant family and continued his religious education until he finished high school, his undergraduate education at Columbia in the 1970s and his graduate work at the University of Chicago brought him into an intellectual world that gave little acknowledgement to his Jewishness. Within the terms of an Enlightenment vision of modernity his Jewishness became a matter of private concern and individual belief. It was disconnected from the public discourses of the university where it was given no intellectual space. Shapiro chose to specialize in the English Renaissance, a culture deeply infused with Christianity.

Not only is his Jewishness silenced but there is an intellectual suppression that organizes a field of secular rationalist intellectual work. As Shapiro recalls

> When I got to graduate school, I was told that there were no Jews, or only a handful, in Shakespeare's England – and so no issues to discuss about the Jews. I was always conscious of what was being suppressed – the discussion of Jews that I was seeing in the texts.
>
> Finally, I realised that I'm both a professor of English and a Jew, and I wanted to know how my people had shaped the culture I was studying.
> [Shapiro, interview in *Chronicle of Higher Education,* 2 February 1996]

This is already an unsettling notion for scholars who have learned to conceive of their Jewishness as a matter of individual religious belief alone. Within the tighter assimilationist terms of a post-war English culture that teaches young Jewish men and women born in England that they need to assimilate into a dominant culture, there is less space than in the ethnic identities of post-war United States.[2]

Shakespeare and the Jews explores how the English in Shakespeare's time focused upon the Jews as a way of exploring troubling questions about themselves. They explored issues of nationhood by considering whether the Jews, without a homeland, could be a nation. The issue of whether the English could be considered a race was often thought about in terms of whether a religious group, like the Jews, had a racial identity. English writers in the sixteenth and seventeenth centuries repeatedly contrasted the Jews to the English. This was often implicitly a gendered discussion relating to masculinities, although Shapiro does not seem to frame it in these terms. Jewish men were said to be effeminate – even to menstruate – while English men were 'manly'; the Jews smelled bad whereas the English were clean.

The writings Shapiro explores seem to return again and again to a deep anxiety about who was and who was not a Jew. This apprehension, in fact, seemed to mask a widespread concern about the stability of English identity. The question he sees obsessing the English was whether the English could lose their own identity and become Jews or take on attributes of Jews. This seemed to be part of the fascination – and revulsion – for a figure like John Traske who was imprisoned in the seventeenth century for founding a sect of Christians who followed some Jewish doctrines. This echoes anxieties that have their source in the long-standing Western denial of the Jewishness of Jesus. This repression was often linked to the demonizing of Jews as 'the other' within the West, where the 'wandering Jew' became a figure of punishment.

In his exploration of *The Merchant of Venice,* Shapiro is concerned to show how the portrayal of Jews would have resonated with contemporary audiences. He goes back to early editions of sources Shakespeare could have drawn from for the story of a Jew demanding a pound of flesh, which link it to male circumcision. Shapiro argues that the story would have provoked widespread fears that a non-Jew could become Jewish. Such questions recur in the play's many allusions to religious conversion. This reflects widespread uncertainties in relation to the stability of English identities. In different periods of upheaval and uncertainty, issues in relation to Jewish identities have been framed in ways that allow for reflections upon the re-visioning of England.

Being Jewish, Being 'English'

Growing up in England in a refugee family that had escaped from continental Europe just before the war was to grow up in the shadows of the Holocaust – the Shoah. In some sense it was to grow up without representation, to be 'invisible'. I was born in England in 1945. I shared with many others the name of 'Victor' for this had been a 'victory' that was to be remembered and celebrated in the streets. After years of a long and difficult war, there was to be a time of peace and reconstruction. England was to be reborn out of the ashes of the blitz and this was a time to look forward, not to dwell on the past. Not only had England been victorious but the 1945 election of a Labour government was to bring into being a period of social justice when the fruits of the peace were to be supposedly shared by all.

I was named after this victory – and as I was named so I was also marked. I carried a public name that carried meaning beyond the personal boundaries of family. But I was also to carry this mark as a sign of protection for it was a promise of what I was to become – 'English', like everyone else – if I could not already be. I was born in Hendon, north London. In those days since I was born in England I was still entitled 'to be English', even though my parents were 'foreign', because they had been born in Poland and in Austria. It was not so easy for them to become English and over 50 years later it can still be difficult for them to feel that they are accepted or that they 'belong'. They were largely self-identified as 'continental' and in many ways they felt separate as a Jewish community. They did not 'speak correctly' in a culture where accent was so important as a social marker, but they felt gratitude for a country that had provided them with refuge, and they did not really want to be reminded about the many who were refused entry before the war when they had nowhere to go.

The established Jewish community was not always welcoming to these 'continentals' who had their own practices and traditions. They were expected to 'fit in' and to accommodate to 'English ways'. The Jews who had come over from Russia and Poland towards the end of the nineteenth century were already on the way to assimilating into a dominant culture. They, and especially their children, were to 'be English', even if they happened to have different religious beliefs. Religion was a matter of individual belief and supposedly did not affect their status as equal citizens. Our parents could not feel so confident in the hopes and aspirations of a liberal culture, for they had experienced the revoking of their rights in Germany and Austria, which had supposedly cherished the ideals of an Enlightenment modernity, even though their families often had the medals to prove the sacrifices they had made in the First World War.[3]

Often there was a silent and unspoken feeling of rejection. They did not speak easily about the communities from which they had come and in which they had felt so integrated. They carried the pain of rejection. At some level this was often transformed in the aspirations they had for their children who were to be 'protected' from the truth of these pains. They were to have their some of own revenge through splitting from their pasts and in feeling that they could give to their children the precious gift of 'becoming English'. But this was also important at another level, for to be English was to be 'safe'. It was this safety that parents were ready to sacrifice for, and it was part of their deep and unquestioned gratitude to England that they also did their best to pass on to their children. They would not have a bad word spoken about England. I remember how difficult it was for them when I went to join an early 'Ban the Bomb' march in 1958 on its way back from Aldermaston. My stepfather, Leo, had learned from his experience at the hands of the Nazis in Germany that Jews should not be involved in politics. As a Jew you had to learn to keep your head down. You were to learn to become 'invisible'. As far as he was concerned you had to learn from the English to behave properly, 'to be seen and not heard'. I was never consciously happy with this message, but it left its mark. It made me careful and at some level it held me back. I learned not to take too many risks.

Our parents, scarred by the horrors of Nazi rule, looked forward to their children 'becoming English'. They felt this was one of the gifts they could offer us. This was part of working for a future and refusing to look back to the past. It was also a way of coping with not being overwhelmed by the sufferings of the recent past. There was a determination to 'make a living' in England so that they could provide their children with those things that they did not have themselves. The children were to 'come first', for they were the future. They allowed you to focus on the future so that you did not have to deal with the past. It was also that 'we', as second-generation children, were to be different from all those Jews, all those uncles, aunts, grandparents, brothers, and sisters who had died in the camps.

This was to be a new beginning and England in the 1950s was to be a land of hope and opportunity in which the past could be left behind. 'We' as children were not to be 'like them', although often we carried the names of the dead, as this was the ancient Jewish custom. We were to know that we were 'English', though somehow, at the same time, we were also supposed to be proud of 'being Jewish'. We were to carry the hopes of our parents for a better life. We were often not allowed to be sad or unhappy or depressed because this threatened to remind them of feelings they did not themselves want to touch. Rather it was our duty somehow to be constantly happy, or at least content, and, if we felt different, we soon learned to keep these unsettling feelings to ourselves.

Naming Identitites

Names matter. But often we carry quite ambivalent feelings about our names and who we might be named after. It can be part of an uncertain family inheritance, especially if, as happened in so many Jewish families, you are named after family members who have died in the Holocaust. This creates its own link and responsibility, but it can produce its own rifts, as in my case, I have a 'public' name that turns me outwards towards the world whilst I also carry an inner name. I was called 'Victor' for the public world. This was a form of self-protection and in the 1950s it was still called my 'Christian' name; but I also carried the name 'Jacob' which was an inner name. It was my Jewish name or my Hebrew name. But it was not necessarily a name that I felt easier with. It remained hidden and was only spoken within the rituals of the synagogue. It remained a private name and at some level I felt uneasy, even shamed, in relation to it.

I did not feel easy about being called 'Victor' because, with the destruction of European Jewry, there was little to celebrate. As far as the Jewish people were concerned, it had not been a victory but a devastating defeat. So it was a name that I carried but one with which I felt it difficult to identify. I soon shortened it to 'Vic', as if I wanted to make myself less visible. As children growing up in the 1950s, we did not really knowingly embody this sense of defeat for we were often left with very ambivalent feelings towards our own Jewishness. It was so much easier to think that we could be English 'like everyone else'. Even in our families we were to be protected from the cruelties of the past. As children we were to represent hope and the future and we were to live without the stains and injuries of the past. This was to protect us as children, but this was also to make things easier for our parents who often found it difficult to speak about what had happened to them. To speak was to make it real and to expose themselves to a pain and sense of loss they often did not want to be reminded of.

The history of the war and of pre-war life in continental Europe was not to be discussed. Even though we inevitably grew up in the shadows of the Shoah, we were not taught to name our experience. Rather, the past was to be passed over in an anxious silence. These histories were often not to be shared, for the sense of rejection and loss they threatened to bring to the surface could not be tolerated. At some level it was as if these histories had not really happened. There was an unspoken anxiety growing up in immigrant Jewish communities in the 1950s that the children 'be normal' and so be 'like everyone else'. If we wondered why we did not have uncles and aunts to visit, we were not told that this was because they had been killed in the Warsaw ghetto, or in Treblinka or Buchenwald. These terrible names were not really to be mentioned in the family, or only in passing. It was just said, as a matter of fact, that we had little extended family. And so as to reassure us, friends of my mother were renamed as 'auntie' so that again we would not feel deprived or inherit a sense of loss. It was important for our parents that we thought of ourselves as having 'happy childhoods' and for us to think that we were not really missing anything that would make us different from other children.

This mystification was even sustained when my father died, in 1950, although I was just five. He had just found out what had happened to his brothers during the war. I felt that he had died from a broken heart, but that was a story that I created for myself. It felt true at some level. These were difficult times, especially for my mother, who had been left with heavy debts. She had to work to support four young children on her own. I felt, then, that being 'without a father' put us in a different situation from other children, especially at school. We learnt not to talk about it. But we still owed it to our mother to 'feel happy', or at least not to allow the inner depression we carried to show. At some level this helped me realize that there was something different about the childhood we had and the tragic circumstances our refugee families had to come to terms with. But I can still find it difficult to fully acknowledge and untie what a particular experience we had as children growing up in the shadows of the Shoah.

Modernity and Jewishness

The idea that, as Jews growing up in England, we were 'like everyone else' was part of the dream of an Enlightenment vision of modernity. We were to grow up into a liberal moral culture that believed that our primary identities were as free and equal rational selves. We were to learn, as Sartre explores it in *Anti-Semite and Jew* to treat Jewishness as if it were contingent and accidental.[4]

An Enlightenment vision of modernity did not in any meaningful sense define 'who' we were as Jews sharing particular histories and cultures, but as part of a tradition of secular rationalism it transformed religion into a subjective matter of individual belief. This is the path towards a universal vision of the rational moral self, which an Enlightenment vision prepared for those Jews who were keen to assimilate. They could leave the restrictions of the ghetto to become free and equal citizens. What is more, they could welcome the Enlightenment as the realization of the universal aspiration of a prophetic Judaism.

In terms of Kant's moral theory, history and culture were deemed to be forms of unfreedom and determination. As we had to learn to 'rise above' inclinations, which reflect an animal nature, to exist as rational moral selves, so we also have to 'rise above' history and culture. We have to learn to think for ourselves as free and autonomous moral agents.[5] So it was that Jewishness became a matter of individual private belief. It had nothing to do with public and civic identities. Within the public realm Jews were to be 'like everyone else' and were to be guaranteed equal legal and political rights. These dreams of modernity still held sway growing up in England in the 1950s. At some level it was as if the Holocaust had not happened.

A dominant English culture had not begun to come to terms with the ways the Holocaust challenges fundamental terms of modernity. The existence of legal and political rights had not proved a guarantee of the humanity of Jews in Nazi Germany. Rights had not been able to secure the human dignity of Jews once these rights could be taken away by the state. This was the crisis that Emmanuel Levinas was responding to, recognizing it as part of a crisis of Western conceptions of modernity. It had to do, in part at least, with the place of ethics within a Greek-defined Western philosophical tradition, and the poverty of liberal ethical traditions that treat ethics subjectively, as a matter of individual opinion alone. Having lived through the Shoah himself, as the defining experience in his life and thought, Levinas recognized the importance of prioritizing ethical responsibilities for others. This was a gift that a Jewish tradition could offer the West and was part of the conflict between Athens and Jerusalem.[6] Jerusalem, properly understood in its relation to Athens could open for us space to acknowledge the priority of ethics over epistemology.

But there was also a recognition, in Levinas, of the ways an Enlightenment vision of modernity, whilst offering a liberal vision of freedom and equality, also worked to weaken Jews' relationships with their own traditions and histories. For in presenting, in Kant's terms, Jewishness as a form of unfreedom and determination, it tended to disavow people's relationship with their own Jewishness. Growing up in post-war England security clearly lay in 'becoming English' and it seemed as if this could only be done through a process of effacing your own Jewishness. Within modernity religion became a matter of individual belief and so of private concern alone. In learning 'to be normal' and 'like everyone else', which were central values within an assimilationist culture, we learnt unconsciously that we were not to be 'visible' as Jews. At some level we were not comfortable in thinking of ourselves as Jews as at all. With Sartre it was easy to feel that it was the anti-Semite who was to do the naming.

Going to Orange Hill, a north London grammar school in the 1950s, even a school with a relatively high proportion of Jewish students who held their own assemblies, it was easy to feel that Jewishness was something to be 'tolerated'. I learned to feel grateful for the tolerance of English society, but this was a tolerance that was often to be paid for in terms of visibility. At some level it was the very lack of public recognition and expression, that worked to make you feel that at some level there was something almost shameful in being Jewish. In school you could feel torn between 'being Jewish' and 'being English', as if there was something automatically suspect about having diverse loyalties. The question was in the air of who you would support in the unlikely circumstance, of a war between England and Israel. It was as if you were called upon to declare yourself and to make a choice.

An earlier generation had known this conflict in a different form. Within the terms of an Enlightenment vision of modernity there should be a straightforward response, that you are 'English', and that you happened to have a different religious practice. This was the clear conviction of German Jews in Weimar Germany. But this vision, and the hopes it carried, was shattered with the rise of Nazism as Jews were gradually marginalized and excluded from civil society. As far as they had been concerned, religious differences only had significance within the private sphere where different religious beliefs were recognized. But English Jews who felt for their 'co-religionists' in worsening conditions in Germany were themselves open to being questioned because they were told that these people who were suffering were Germans or Poles while they were 'English'. So English Jews could feel that they had to hide their feelings for what was going on. They could be made to feel that it was 'wrong' for them to feel so angry and hurt.

Modernity established a firm distinction between public and private spheres. Within the public sphere of citizenship individuals existed as free and equal rational selves. It was only in the private sphere of family that difference was acknowledged, and then only as individual differences of belief. As Jews we were supposedly 'invisible' in public where we were to be 'like everyone else' whilst in the private sphere of the family we were supposed to somehow 'be Jewish'. It is this split between private and public, between family and school that is so familiar to different generations of refugee and immigrant children. The ease with which you learn to 'switch', often assuming different identities within these different spheres, makes it almost automatic. But you also learn to police these boundaries and you can feel uneasy when school friends come home. I can still feel some of the tension. I can also appreciate the efforts my mother went to to provide an abundance of food, as if to compensate for any grounds of unease.

As children we often spoke better English than our parents and we could feel unease whenever parents came into school because of their accent. As soon as boundaries were transgressed we could feel anxious. We were living in England but as children we had to learn for ourselves how to 'become English'. This was not something parents could pass on to us. Often this meant watching other pupils at school and at some level adapting and imitating their behaviours. We learnt to conform from the outside towards the inner, first adapting to behaviours in the hope that 'English' feelings would somehow follow. We learned to identify and suppress aspects of a Jewish difference that might draw attention and so prove that we were 'other' than what we were presenting ourselves to be. Living out the dreams and aspirations of modernity, we were concerned with the machinery of turning difference into 'the same'. We did not want to be difference. We wanted to be 'like everyone else' and we were often more than ready to pay the price.

Double Consciousness/Silent Identities

Growing up within the Jewish refugee community in north-west London, we often had a limited sense of our parents as 'refugees'. We often had little idea of where they had come from, especially if it was from a country like Poland that existed behind an 'iron curtain'. It was as if Poland existed in an imaginary space of its own. Warsaw was not a capital we could think of visiting, even if Vienna was. We were living in a relatively prosperous middle-class community. This is where we were to belong, not asking how our families had settled there. In London in the 1950s, to be different was to stick out and so to 'be abnormal' and this created its own fear. As Jews, we did not want to be different but we desperately wanted to be 'like everyone else'. Often it was important for us, as children, to remind ourselves that 'we were born in England so we must be 'English'. The logic seemed incontrovertible and so reassuring.

As children we learnt about the war and we were told about the Nazis but often this was in generalized terms, sometimes as an early warning against thinking we could marry anyone who was not Jewish. As Anne Karpf has said recently 'other children were told stories about monsters, goblins and wicked witches; we learnt about the Nazis'.[7]

We learned but often we were not told directly. It was a threat that was there in the background of everyday life to be mentioned at times, but not really to be explained. Often we learnt about what had happened to the Jews during the war through seeing the same newsreel images of dead bodies as anyone else. Often the images were overwhelming and very little was said about them. It was left to us to imagine that these images could somehow be our uncles and aunts. It was too terrifying – and it only came much later in adult years – to recognize that they could also be our cousins. We did not want to let these images in, because they threatened the sense we needed of living a 'normal' and 'happy' childhood.

Often we learned to watch in silence, feeling uneasy for our parents, in some way instinctively wanting to protect them. We learned not to expect the adults to say much. It was as if we had already absorbed their pain unconsciously as the second generation. At some level we knew that, whatever they had suffered, they had suffered more than enough. It was our task to somehow redeem their lives, make things better for them. This could be partly an unconscious drive to do well and succeed at school. It took different forms. We did not want to let them down or disappoint them but at some level we learned not to expect very much from them also. For many of them found it difficult to give emotionally, after the rejections, terror and loss that they had experienced in their own lives. They had been separated from their parents at a young age and often had not received the love they needed. Somehow it was our task as children to make it good for them. We knew the wounds could not be healed, but at least we could learn to expect very little for ourselves. Often we learned to be responsible before it was time. Many children in the second generation learned to look after their own parents, automatically forsaking their own needs. This could seem the least they could do.

As children we learned not to ask about the war and what had happened to the wider family. We learnt that our parents 'had suffered enough'. We learnt to hide and conceal our own unhappiness and depression from them, for we did not want to add to their pain. Rather we learnt to collude in the idea that we 'had a happy childhood' and that as children we had 'everything we could want'. I even learned to believe this when my father died, somehow colluding in the notion that, as children, 'we were too young to know' so that we did not need to mourn for ourselves. We had to learn to exercise grief in the privacy of our own dreams, but children often learn to blame themselves and it was easy for me to promise in my dreams that 'I would be good' if only my dad would come back.

The question that at some level haunted our childhoods, although it was rarely articulated, was how did our parents survive when so many people perished? What entitled them to live when so many died? This question was often too difficult and painful to voice for the adults, so it was unconsciously passed on to the second generation. But it was not a question that we could ask anyone; rather it was left hanging. Sometimes it was a question whose presence we were not consciously aware of. But it could be part of the unspoken pressure to achieve in whatever arena, to prove that we are somehow entitled to live. Not only did we have to prove our own entitlement but somehow we had to redeem and make good the broken lives of our parents. Again this was not something that was consciously demanded. It could be expressed in a look of disappointment. That was more than enough.

Growing up in a refugee family in the 1950s was often not to consciously be aware that our families were refugees. This was yet another truth that from which we were to be protected. It might be something that we knew intellectually, but not really emotionally. This also reflected the unease that parents felt about accepting their sense of rejection from countries they felt so identified with. There was often an unspoken hurt and feeling of betrayal. It could not easily be talked about because of the feelings it threatened to bring to the surface. It was easier often to reject the country of origin, rather than to come to terms with your own difficult feelings of rejection. This did not stop us celebrating every birthday with a rich Viennese chocolate cake. I just assumed that this was what all families did. Only much later did I recognize where these customs came from.

Anglo-Jewry in the 1950s was in many ways a frozen, traumatized community that had not really begun to come to terms with the Shoah. Kitty Hart, a child refugee, described in her *Return to Auschwitz* how quickly she learned on arrival in England not to talk, even to her closest family, about her camp experience. She was told by her uncle that people would just not want to know and you did not want to embarrass them.[8] She kept her silence until the 1970s and her own family were grown up, before she started to share some of her experience. Post-war England wanted to turn its back on the sufferings of the war and did not want to be reminded of what happened to European Jewry. Life was to 'get back to normal' and people were looking towards a new future. They did not want to be reminded of the horrors of the past – or only in the heroic terms of the movies.

The refugees who lived in England throughout the war learnt to 'fit in' as best they could. They were to learn to talk English and make their own contributions to the war effort, if they were not imprisoned as 'enemy aliens' on the Isle of Man. There was a sense in which 'they came from nowhere and did not really have a past'. They had been uprooted, as Simone Weil describes it, in both space and time.[9]

Their energies were to be given over to making a living as best they could. So it was hardly surprising if we felt strangely suspended and unrooted as children, doing our best to root ourselves in often not very hospitable English manners and customs. It was easy to feel that, whatever we did, we were somehow 'not right' – our noses were too big or we talked too emotionally with our hands. We learned to contain ourselves, for often it fell to us as children to mediate between your parents and the host community. At some level, despite everything we did and the efforts we made, we could feel ourselves outsiders.

This is why it was so exciting when Colin Wilson published *The Outsider* in the late 1950s. It helped to name a significant feeling, even if it was very different from his intention, and it gave some acceptability to it. Years before post-modernism it created a limited space for difference and named a tradition of double consciousness. The assimilationist English culture was still very much intact, but there were some new spaces opening up. It could help to make us, as children of refugees, a little more self-accepting, a little easier and less judgmental on ourselves.

Identity and Difference

It was in the 1960s that the cracks in modernity were beginning to show. With the influx of an Afro-Caribbean population and the racism that the community met in terms of jobs and housing, there were others who were not going to be able to live out their dreams of the 'mother country'. The high expectations were soon dashed and the realities of life in England, which was so resistant to the notion of a multicultural community, were often hard and oppressive. Even if people wanted to 'become English', they were not going to be allowed to do so. It took time to recognize that it was not simply an issue of individual prejudice but that there was institutionalized racism that had to be confronted. It was a matter of undoing the link not only between 'being English' and 'being Christian' that the Jewish community had to confront but also between 'being English' and 'being white'. Historically there had also been the issue of whether Jews were 'white' and in earlier times they were not allowed to be, even if they wanted this. Whiteness was tied up with the conditions of modernity.

An Enlightenment vision of modernity had insisted that 'the other' could be made like 'the same'. Underlying differences there was, supposedly, the shared reality of existing as rational selves. As rational selves individuals were guaranteed equal legal and political rights within the public realm, but this Cartesian vision was already gendered and racialized. It was a dominant white, Christian, heterosexual masculinity that alone could take its reason for granted. Modernity had in a crucial sense encoded a secularized Christian tradition in its antagonism to the body and sexuality as 'the sins of the flesh'. A dominant rationalist tradition, as Nietzsche recognized, showed how the body and sexuality as part of an 'animal nature' had been superseded. Reason was set in categorical distinction to nature, and women, Jews, and people of colour were deemed to be 'closer to nature'. They were deemed, in different ways, to be less rational so that they could not take their 'humanity' for granted.

As Christianity had supposedly 'superseded' Judaism, as Daniel Boyarin has it, the disembodied spirit had superseded 'Carnal Israel', so within modernity, the mind was to control the body.[10] The identification of Judaism with the body, sexuality and 'carnality' was central to the anti-Semitic discourses of the West. This helped to produce its own forms of Jewish self-hatred, as Sander Gillman has explored it. A crucial text in this cultural history is Otto Weininger's influential *Sex and Character*. Identifying himself with a Kantian universalism and its radical separation of reason from nature, Weininger could only disdain his own homosexuality and Jewishness, as signs of a lesser and flawed moral particularity. Suicide was the only way out for him. He could find no root to validating the body as a form of knowledge. Rather he came to see himself through the dominant Christian eyes of the West and there was no space open for him to come to terms with either his homosexuality or his Jewishness. Rather this only confirmed, in his own eyes, the cultural identification of

Jewish men as feminine.[11] The cultural and political language of minorities often fails to recognize the ease with which 'others' come to see themselves through the eyes of the dominant culture. As Simone Weil viewed it, this is part of the workings of power. This is also something that Franz Fanon grapples with in *Black Skin, White Mask* when he looks into the mirror and has got to come to terms with his negative feelings about his own black body. His body stands as a reminder of the 'uncivilized' and he has unknowingly been brought up within a colonial culture to despise it.[12] He shares his inner struggle to shift his attitude and feelings about his body and so about himself. Here is an inner link between the internalized oppression of racism and the Jewish self-hatred that Gillman explores in *Jewish Self-Hatred*. Often these struggles take place away from the gaze of the public sphere. In public people often learn to hide these inner struggles and present themselves in more acceptable ways.[13]

With feminism learning from the movements for black consciousness and black power in the 1960s in the United States about the importance of re-evaluating experience, not only intellectually but also emotionally, different ways of theorizing the relationship between the personal and the political came into focus. Women refused to see themselves and evaluate their experience through the eyes of a dominant heterosexual masculinity. With post-modernism in the 1990s there has been a greater appreciation of a politics of difference and a developing unease about talking of 'women' as a generalized category. If discourse theory as a theoretical tendency can help us identify subaltern voices that have been suppressed and marginalized within dominant theoretical discourses, often it remains within a rationalist framework. Its attention to the multiplicity of voices within texts can also help to show 'the jew' as a floating signifier within a variety of different literary texts.[14]

We can be made aware of the variety of meanings attached to the notion of 'the jew', so helping us question what is often taken to be a 'naive' assumption in relation to too homogenized a vision of 'the jew'. It is only through the display of meanings within a particular literary text that we can say what meaning is being given to 'the jew', but this literary practice, alive as it is to the multiplicities of deferred meanings, involves its own forms of denial. As with Lyotard's discussion of 'the jew', which this discourse work often draws on, it finds it difficult to give adequate recognition to the historical realities of anti-Semitism and to the diverse religious and spiritual traditions of the Jews as a people.[15] It unwittingly serves to silence this discussion, as it too often gets caught in a circle of representations. It is just this circle that Levinas helps to break in his recognition of ethical obligations to the other.

Modernity is still to be named as a secularized Christian project in its rationalist disdain for the body, sexualities and emotional life. If recent post-modern work has sought to give belated recognition to the body and emotional life as sources of knowledge, it has too often focused upon the play of meanings within texts. This makes it difficult to recognize *how* racism and anti-Semitism are entwined within the terms of modernity. In more recent years young Jews have learnt from young black men and women to rethink issues of identity, ethnicity and difference in the context of revisioning Britain. The notion that 'black is beautiful' involved a re-evaluation of what has so easily been devalued and despised. As young Afro-Caribbean men and women have also had to come to terms with slavery, without being limited by it, so young Jewish men and women have demanded the space to come to terms with the Shoah, without limiting Jewish identities to this experience. These explorations are shared in art and literature as they are in the cinema. Jewish film festivals have been significant in sharing these representations.

When there is a sharp break and dislocation between generations, as there was for the Jewish refugees fleeing Nazi rule, there are few stories and nursery rhymes that can be passed on. The past has been tainted and it needs to be left behind. If the children are to 'become English', how can parents sing to them in Yiddish? This language was already devalued in the eyes of the Enlightened Jews of Germany and Austria as not a 'real' language. This is a sadness that a younger generation is recognizing for it breaks what could be a vital link to the pre-war Jewish cultures of Poland, Russia, and Lithuania. Unless such traditions can somehow be recovered in a different context, what stories are we to tell and what songs are we to sing to our children? How are they to learn to feel good about themselves as Jews, as well as feel good about themselves as English, Scottish or Welsh?

We might be able to celebrate the new hybrid identities that are being created, but we must not minimize the pain that is often experienced as young people feel torn between different cultural inheritances. The high rate of young Asian women, for instance, who have committed suicide should make us more aware of the emotional and material difficulties that people have to endure, before they can feel at ease with themselves in these new settings. A revisioning of Britain, which allows recognition for a multi-cultural society will necessarily offer more cultural space than was available in the 1950s. With post-modernism there is a greater theoretical space for the exploration of diverse identities and the creation of new hybrid identities, but often we identify with freedom before we have really understood the complex attachments to culture and tradition.

If these are automatically to be defined in negative terms, we need to refigure Enlightenment notions of modernity.

Too often modernity has insisted upon the effacing of cultural and ethnic difference. If I have an obligation to recognize another face to face, as Levinas has it, this has to be a recognition that validates and affirms the other person's difference. When I face others, do I face them as Victor? What difference does it make if I face them as Jacob? For years this has been a hidden Jewish name, though it was also a name carried with some pride. But it could also be a name that was shamed and it takes time to feel pride for what has been culturally shamed. This is an issue of self worth and dignity with which people of colour, gays, and lesbians have long struggled.

As they have learned from their own bitter experience, the issue is not exclusively a matter of what representations are available in the broader culture, important as this is, but also *how* do we want to voice our own histories or herstories. For a second generation that has grown up in the shadows of the Shoah, it has been a matter of learning *how* they might learn 'to face' the Shoah and whether they can find a voice at all in the face of the pain and terror of that suffering. It has also been a question – one with which Rosenzweig and Levinas have struggled – of whether you can speak out of the vitality of a living Jewish tradition within contemporary cultures. This has to be part of a revisioning of Britain as much as it has to be part of a reframing of what has been so easily talked about as 'Christian' Europe.

Re-visionings

Why does it still feel so difficult to talk more personally about these questions of Jewish identities in an academic setting – to share these personal as well as theoretical reflections? Is it because at some level I still feel that there is something shameful and that I fear being rejected if I share some of these feelings? Is this fear of rejection in the particular form that it takes linked to masculinity, as Jewish feminists seem more easily to blend the personal with the theoretical? Are there particular issues that come into play within modernity when it comes to speaking about Jewish masculinities? It is as if, within modernity, you can only prove that you are a 'man enough' if you are ready to be silent about your Jewishness. For there is almost a contradiction in terms bringing 'Jewish' and 'man' together, for there is a culturally entrenched notion within modernity that Jewish men are 'really' feminine. This is a fear we talked about in relation to Weininger. This means that they are somehow 'pretending' to be other than what they are.

This links in complex ways to the issue of being exposed or 'found out', a sense that, at some level, being Jewish, you are somehow already guilty and that if people would somehow discover that you are Jewish they would show you to the door. So, for a particular generation of post-Holocaust Jews, you learn to automatically conceal your Jewish identity, unless you feel safe to reveal it. This links to a fear of being 'found out', even though you might not have the slightest feeling what this refers too. This connects to the familiar feelings, reproduced within the terms of modernity, that if people came to know that you are Jewish then they will reject you, so you had better keep this particular piece of information to yourself. This becomes so automatic as part of a process of self-policing that you are barely aware you are doing it. The fear, so present for the second generation, is that you will not be 'safe' and that it is best to keep yourself hidden and concealed.

For example, when I turned up on Sunday morning in July a few years ago to give an early draft of this chapter as a paper to an academic conference on these themes, I was very politely told that I had been taken off the programme. They had tried to reach me for the last two weeks and had not been able to contact me, so they had assumed that I no longer wanted to do the paper. This made me feel very uneasy and part of me felt that I should just leave there and then. Part of me also knew that I had wanted to contact the organizers but had not really felt the need, because I was on the last draft of the programme that was sent out. But at some unconscious level I was struck that it probably also had to do with my unease about talking about some of these issues directly and personally within an academic conference. I know that the suggestion for the paper had been warmly welcomed by the organizers, but this did not stop me feeling uneasy.

It was as if these issues should not be 'talked about' in public, that it was too risky and too dangerous. At some level I was also ambivalent about doing it at all since this was also the first time I was speaking in such a setting on such themes. As Sarah Sceats who had helped in the organization picked up, there had also been some difficulties with other papers that were to address similar themes.[14] [I originally gave an earlier draft of this chapter to the conference on 'Re-Visioning England' that was held at the university of Kingston in July 1996.] But once I had begun to talk I felt a lot easier. I felt as if is some kind of load had lifted and I felt a little fuller in myself. The discussion it provoked was interesting and fruitful and it seemed to help focus some important questions. But it also made me feel a little 'odd' for it somehow confirmed in public that I had a 'different' past and that I was forced to deal with issues in my growing up that seemed to feel quite 'strange' to many people. It was as if a 're-visioning' of England, and of what it could mean to be 'English', was going on in the room.

At the same time as I was talking about a Jewish childhood in which I wanted 'to be normal' and 'like everyone else' – and this is also how I partly felt about myself as an internal experience – it was also difficult to live in public with the 'strangeness' of the history that I was sharing. It was if I had to meet myself in a different way in public, possibly for the first time. But in many ways it also helped me explain different things I have felt in the past. From now on I think it is going to be a little 'easier' and I will feel a little more at ease with myself and with my Jewishness. It is part of a process of 'coming out' as Jewish. I do not think it will be easy but it will be easier.

This also reflects a difficulty with many contemporary discussions of hybridity, which tend to assume that it is much easier for people to feel 'at ease' with their different cultural, 'racial', and ethnic his/herstories than they do. Often it is difficult to reconcile the different experiences and traditions that we carry and this shows itself in what we are ready to share and show to others. The feelings of shame and unease can be carried in relation to class, sexualities, 'race', ethnicities, which can remain unspoken, but go quite deep. This is why we need ways of imagining different levels of peoples' experience and the complex ways they relate to available discourses and representations. Often we have ways of defending ourselves against feelings of unease and we become so used to strategies of denial that we cannot identify them for what they are. We have to be wary of remaining trapped theoretically within the play of appearances.

As we went for lunch a young Irishman pulled me aside to say how much he had got from the session. He told me that, just the week before, his mother had come down to Dublin to spend an evening with him. They had shared a bottle of wine. This had almost never happened before and he sensed that she had something to tell him. She wanted to tell him about his middle name. He had two and one was acknowledged as Huguenot and talked about in the family but the other was Jewish. He heard for the first time that his maternal grandmother had been Jewish. This was unsettling to the sense of identity that he carried. He had always carried the second middle name but never really knew what it meant. 'It was just a name', or so he had thought.

But it was proving very helpful for him to know about this naming for it made a number of things clearer to him. He had always felt very much at ease with Jewish friends and he had often wondered why this should be so. He had found himself with close Jewish friends at different times in his life. It is easy to think of this as a 'coincidence' but it raises questions – questions we have difficulty thinking about within a rationalist culture about hidden/buried identities and what it is we can be said to 'carry' from our ancestors. This is something that African traditions have little difficulty with, but even with the openings of post-colonial literatures we often refuse to validate traditional forms of knowledge. It could be said, in Benjamin's terms, that some 'space' had been filled out in his aura with this new information that his mother had passed on to him. She felt the urgency to make a special visit. She recognized that this was significant information that she had withheld and that, in a sense, he had a right to know. It was significant if he was to revision his identity.

Knowing a little more of where he had come from, he also knew a little more about 'who' he was. Within a homogenized vision of England, these knowledges have been long suppressed. People did not often want to recover the complexities of 'their' English identities. This was a way they controlled their anxieties about Englishness, so often played out in relation to the Jews. This is not simply a matter of available knowledge, for you have to be ready to 'hear' what is being said. He could have rejected the gifts his mother had brought with her. This is part of a process that cannot be forced, nor is it a matter of will. Often it is a matter of taking the next step when you are ready for it.

Someone else also came up who was of Irish background, although this had been barely acknowledged through his growing up. His mother had done her best to present herself as 'English', but now it felt important to him to explore his Irish inheritance. This was part of a felt knowledge about himself, although he could not really explain it. He just knew in some way that this was something that he needed to do for himself. This was not simply a matter of reframing experience in terms of a different discourse. Rather it opens up difficult issues about the relationship of language to experience.

Such responses often follow the breaking of a silence and they are heartening when they are made. But often these realizations remain at odds with the dominant ways we theorize identities within contemporary theoretical frameworks. It is these traditions that also have to be shifted if we are to bring light to bear upon complex identities that have for so long been denied and shamed. This is a crucial part of the re-visioning of England. Often it has been in the darkness of the cinema or in the privacy of reading literature, that some of these connections are being made. It has been through extending the realm of imagination that we have also been able to voice aspects of our his/herstories that have for so long been repressed in the name of an England that has long past. It was also in this spirit that I wanted to return to Poland with Anna, my partner, to confront some of these shadows in our own individual and shared journeys through life.

Notes

1. James Shapiro not only helps to explode the myth of the absent Jew but, more significantly explores how literature conveys such notions. *Shakespeare and the Jews* (New York, Columbia University Press, 1996).
2. For some understandings of the politics of assimilation see, for instance, Robert Bellah, *The Broken Covenant: American Civil Religion in Time of Trial* (New York, Seabury Press, 1975) and Robert Bellah, Richard Madsen, William M Sullivan, Ann Swidler, and Steven M. Tipton, *Habits of the Heart: Middle America Observed* (London, Hutchinson, 1988); Steven M. Cohen, *American Assimilation or Jewish Revival?* (Bloomington, Indiana University Press, 1988) and Charles E. Silberman, *A Certain People* (New York, Summit, 1985).
3. For an illuminating discussion of the predicaments that an Enlightenment vision of modernity presented Jews and Jewishness in different historical and cultural contexts, see Zygmunt Bauman, *Modernity and Ambivalence* (Cambridge, Polity, 1993).
4. Jean-Paul Sartre in *Anti-Semite and Jew* explores how a universalism that was identified with an Enlightenment vision of modernity, which treated individuals as instantiations of rational selves, served implicitly to devalue Jewishness that came to be treated as a form of particularism (New York, Schocken Books, 1968).
5. I have explored these themes within Kantian ethics and the tensions that remain unresolved in relation to liberal conceptions of respect and injustice in *Kant, Respect and Injustice: The Limits of Liberal Moral Theory* (London, Routledge, 1986).
6. For some interesting essays that help to reflect upon differences between Athens and Jerusalem, see Emmanuel Levinas, *Difficult Freedom: Essays on Judaism* (London, The Athlone Press, 1990). For some helpful background discussion see, Susan A. Handelman, *Fragments of Redemption: Jewish Thought and Literary Theory* (Bloomington, Indiana University Press, 1991).

7. Ann Karpf's parents survived the Nazi Holocaust and came to Britain in 1947. She has explored the profound impact of her parents' wartime experience on her daily life in *The War After* (London, Minerva, 1997).

8. Kitty Hart has shared her experience of arriving in England as a child survivor just after the close of the war, and her later visit to Auschwitz with her children in *Return To Auschwitz* (London, Sidgwick & Jackson, 1981).

9. Simone Weil explores diverse aspects of an experience of uprootedness in a text that she was writing for the liberation of France, *The Need For Roots* (London, Routledge & Kegan Paul, 1972).

10. Daniel Boyarin has done very significant work exploring how some of the different visions which inform Judaism and Christianity in relation to the body and sexuality help to explain the difficult historical relationship between them. See *Carnal Israel: Reading Sex in Talmudic Judaism* (Berkeley, University of California Press, 1993).

11. Otto Weininger, *Sex and Character* (London, William Heinemann, 1906) had an enormous impact in Vienna when it was first published. In different ways it influenced both Freud and Wittgenstein.

12. Franz Fanon, *Black Skin, White Mask* (London, Pluto Books, 1984) shares his history of growing up in Martinique and moving to Paris as a medical student. He explores the ways he is forced to come to terms with his blackness, body, and sexuality. It is a striking work of black consciousness that learns from Sartre's reflections on Jewishness in *Anti-Semite and Jew* (New York, Schocken Books, 1960).

13. Sander Gillman, *Jewish Self-Hatred,* explores diverse traditions of Jewish ambivalence and self loathing within modernity. (Baltimore, Johns Hopkins University Press, 1989).

14. Bryan Cheyette and Laura Marcus have edited an interesting collection, *Modernity, Culture and the Jew* (Cambridge, Polity, 1998), which helps to explore the figure of 'the jew' at the heart of different versions of modernity and postmodernity as well as challenging post-modern revisions of modernity which have tended to locate Jews in a dominant Judeo-Christian tradition.

15. For a sense of Jean Francois Lyotard's discussion see *Heidegger and 'the jews'* (Minneapolis: University of Minnesota Press, 1990). I have explored some of the tensions in Lyotard's work in 'Identity, Memory and Difference': Lyotard and 'the Jews', in *The Politics of Jean-Francois Lyotard: Justice and Political Theory* (ed.) Chris Rojek, Bryan Turner (London, Routledge, 1998).

Broken Histories

Beginnings

I want to relate a history that is both personal yet shared by many who have learned to think of themselves as part of a 'second generation' of Jews, recognizing crucial differences that remain to be explored between children of survivors of Nazi concentration and extermination camps and children of those who were refugees from Nazi Europe.

As I grew up in a refugee family in north-west London, which had fled from Nazi-occupied Europe, it was difficult to imagine where my parents had come from. I knew that they had come from somewhere else, as I have mentioned, and that they thought of themselves as 'continental', but I was not very clear about their origins. We did not talk very much about it and there was a sense that too much knowledge could prove dangerous. There was also a clear sense that we, as four boys born in London, were to become 'English'. We were told that we were English because we were born in London, and that no one could take this away from us, but at some level our parents knew that this was not completely true for they had had their own citizenship revoked by the Nazis and been forced to leave countries they had grown up to love and with which they had grown to identify.

With the end of the war there was to be a new beginning. Our parents thought that one of their responsibilities as parents was to protect us from the past. They thought that we did not need to know what had happened to them or where they had come from because this could only make it more difficult to 'become English'. Their task was to protect us from history and somehow to make us feel 'at home' in the present. We were to be a new beginning, for we represented their hopes for a different and more peaceful future. It was very important for these refugee families to have children and, in the beginning, my mother did not find it easy. She had to wait before being able to conceive but when she started having children she could not stop. She had four boys in quick succession.

We were to carry neutral first names to make the transition into English society easier. My older brother was called John and I was named Victor to identify with the days of victory after the Second World War. But if the end of the war was a moment of relief it was hardly a moment of victory for, as Jews, we had to come to terms with the destruction of European Jewry. Nearly everyone on my father's side had perished in the camps. On my mothers side, her mother and brother were the only people to find safety. Her father had fled east to die in a camp.

At the end of the war there was a great deal of uncertainty about what had happened to relatives. Had they been able to escape or had they perished in Treblinka and Auschwitz? We were born into these uncertainties as our parents desperately sought for news about what had happened. There were endless inquiries and false hopes. My father's family had come from Warsaw. He was the youngest of five brothers and he was the only one to have been out of Poland when the German forces invaded on 1 September 1940. He was in England, in relative safety, but his brothers and their families were all in Warsaw. He still had hopes that they might have survived in hiding, for he knew that some of them at least were hiding in the Aryan part of Warsaw. As we were to find out later, one brother had died in the ghetto and two brothers had perished in Treblinka. A fourth brother, Chaim, was in hiding with his surviving sisters-in law and their children.

This was not clear to us at the end of the war, and my father probably lived in hope that they had somehow survived. Again this is speculation – an attempt to fill an empty space. Little of this was to be talked about. Instead, the children were to be protected from these anxieties and it was thought that we were 'too young to understand'. It was felt that if we were not told then we could not be affected by what was going on around us. Our parents often considered that it was to be their supreme duty to be positive whenever they talked to the children. This was something I only recognized years later when my older brother, Johnny, died of cancer at the age of 37. It was a terrible time for the family but some of my mother's refugee friends assumed that their task was somehow to remain 'positive' in the face of so much sadness. My mother felt a need to concentrate all the mourning in herself and she found it difficult to recognize the feelings of others, even those closest to my brother. She found it hard to deal with my own grief and I soon realized that I had to find a separate space of my own to grieve. At the same time she would blame others for somehow not grieving. This kind of double bind was all too familiar from our childhood. At some level, it was as if we could not exist for ourselves as children, and that we existed simply in relation to our parents' hopes and aspirations for us.

We often learned, as children, that at some level we owed it to our parents to be happy and 'normal'. Often we embodied the anxieties and uncertainties that surrounded us as children. We lived in an atmosphere of tension and uncertainty, but we could not talk about it. There were few words. We learned that our parents had 'suffered enough' but at the same time they felt guilt at having survived at all. Why had they survived when so many perished? It was not that they were good or that they somehow had deserved to survive. They knew that they had been lucky or that they had had wealth and connections that made it possible for them to leave when so many others could not. They had had to make their own compromises with fate but these stories were rarely shared.

My mother told of how she had gone into the Gestapo headquarters in Vienna to request permission to leave. This was, in fact, something that was possible but the Nazis were shocked that any Jewish woman should exercise this right. We learned of this courage and as children admired it. We heard less of the fears and anxieties – we were to be protected from these feelings.

We were to learn not to talk about the past. Often we were asked 'what do you know about suffering?' in a way that taught us to control our own sadness, anger, and disappointments. Sometimes it was difficult to voice our experience within our families without feeling that we were unsettling a precarious balance. Often we were told that we were 'only children' and we could not understand. Often this was a way for parents to protect themselves from their own histories.

As silence fell on the past, so families learned to look towards the future, especially towards the children who were supposed to 'have everything that they could want' and that their parents could afford. Our parents often looked to us to provide them with a sense of future. They wanted us to fulfil dreams that they had been unable to realize in their own lives. They wanted us to succeed, but they also wanted us to be 'normal', to 'fit in' with the English culture in which they had found refuge.

Our parents looked to us to redeem their histories. We were to provide the validation for their survival. At the same time we owed it to them to be happy and to be 'like everyone else'. These were conflicting demands for we were to be 'proud' of being Jewish but we were not to make too much of this. We were to learn not to draw attention to ourselves as Jews. Rather we were to be Jewish in private, when it had to do with the family and the synagogue, but we were to adapt and accommodate in public. We learned to cross these boundaries with ease, adapting to what was expected from us. As we could not learn how to be 'English' from the family we had to watch carefully and observe at school. We had to learn from the other boys what it meant to be English boys and conform to the behaviour that was expected of us. This helped to produce a particular kind of sensitivity and double consciousness that is all too familiar to the marginalized.[1]

There was a widespread sense of gratitude amongst the refugee population towards England and its institutions that could not be easily questioned. There was little sense that England could have done more to save Jews, or to provide a haven in a time of need.

Jewish men knew that they had to make a living in order to support their wives and children. This became the priority for them. They worked hard to make money, and they expected not to be questioned. Often they were absent figures in the family who took great pride in their children, but their everyday relationships with their children were often remote. Children largely became the responsibility of the women, as was the general pattern in middle-class 1950s Britain.

'Like Everyone Else'

As children we often wanted to become English, and not just because this was what our parents expected from us (to ease their own transition in a new culture). We watched others for signs of how we should behave. We learned to avoid behaving in ways that might draw attention to differences. If Jews were emotional and learned to talk with their hands, we would learn to be reserved and would be careful not to use our hands. But this was to internalize unknowingly certain anti-Semitic stereotypes of Jewishness. It was at odds with the pride that we were supposed to feel about being Jewish in private. Here, again, was the pervasive demarcation between private and public. The lines were drawn, and we learned to police them. I remember the anxiety when non-Jewish friends used to come home, as I have said, and the efforts that went into getting the food right. Often these were difficult boundaries to cross and we felt easier when the lines were maintained.

I grew up wanting to be 'like everyone else'. Great efforts went into fitting in and being accepted at school. This meant that Jewishness became largely a private matter to do with home and family. We did not want to be different, for the 1950s witnessed a drive towards assimilation. This had been important because 'becoming English' became the way of securing our safety. If there were sacrifices to be made in the public expression of Jewishness, then this is a price that we were more than ready to pay. We learned to look to the future at the same time as we split from the past. When my older brother was born in July 1944 and I was born in December 1945 we were also given Jewish names that linked us to the family. Jewish families often name people after relatives who have died, so sustaining a soul connection with ancestors. It was with the birth of the twins in 1948 that my father and mother had finally come to accept the death of their families, and they were named after my father's brothers who had died in Warsaw. The link with the past was to be honoured, but it was rarely to be spoken about in the present.

It can still be difficult for me to recognize that the family histories I carry as part of the second generation are different from the histories of many friends. I so wahted to be 'like everyone else' that I learned to believe that my background was very little different from those of others. I had shaped my experience to be 'normal' and had learned to believe my mother's view that, as children, we had everything we had wanted. This myth of a 'happy childhood' went along with the myth of normality. Because I did not want to be different, at some level I did not really want to know about the very different histories my family had or to experience the loss. We lived without an extended family but this was also true of many of the families that we knew. It took time before I could think out the significance of the absence of family or really ask why we didn't have more cousins to play with. This was all part of living abnormal 'normal' lives.

At some level we learned to fear the revelation of our natures, for we did not want to recognize our Jewishness where it was not appropriate. This meant learning a particular form of self-control and self-discipline in relation to emotional life. In a culture of assimilation the standards are set by the dominant English culture and we learned to participate in our own ways. We might learn to mouth the hymns in school assemblies whilst not actually singing them. We recognized that we were different as Jews and wanted to remain loyal to our own traditions, even if these were given little public recognition at the time. This was a period when there were still nativity plays in schools at Christmas time and Jewish children might be given marginal roles so that they did not feel *too* excluded. We might be the shepherds rather than Joseph.

A Fear of Difference

Even now, in my fifties, I sometimes feel that I should somehow feel the same as others. I can still find it difficult to come to terms with my particular Jewish history. Sometimes I am struck, when I share some of my history with others, at how different it feels from their own experience.

At some level this has to do with a fear of difference, for I can feel too vulnerable, too exposed. There is a tension between an intellectual acknowledgement that I might give to difference, and the ways I feel emotionally about my Jewishness. Of course this is part of a changing process familiar to new generations of immigrants and refugees but it is striking how compartmentalized I can still keep my life. I can still feel anxious about bringing the different pieces together. I have learned to talk more easily about Jewish difference at work, teaching in the sociology department at Goldsmiths College, University of London – this has become easier as I have grown to feel more secure and less irrationally threatened in my position. For years I was haunted by a sense of not really belonging, as if I could somehow be asked to leave at any moment. Paradoxically, this is something I share with first-year students who often feel that they might be 'discovered' and told that it has all been a mistake and they should not really be at university after all. Of course, finally becoming a professor, when I shared issues of Jewish identity and memory after Auschwitz in my inaugural, has made this all easier.

It is interesting to think about whether I am 'Jewish' at work. At some level a culture of assimilation has left its mark and I live partially, at least, in hiding. I am careful about where and how I might share myself. I am watchful of people's responses and often quick to withdraw if I feel an inappropriate response. It is as if I am quicker to sense people's responses than they are themselves. At some unspoken level I am still wary of being 'too Jewish', because this is what I often felt as a graduate student in philosophy. I was made too feel 'too emotional' and more engaged in ideas than was usual. As I still wanted to be 'like everyone else' I was careful to police my own responses. I learned to write for myself and to honour spaces where I could express more of my own experience. Eventually, in the early 1970s, these emotional issues took me into psychotherapy. I was uncertain about traditional forms of psychoanalysis and more interested in expressive forms of therapy, for this is what I sensed that I needed for myself to grow and develop.[2]

If these alternative psychotherapies helped me to explore different aspects of my familial history, they were often not attuned to the historical and the cultural. The theories on which they are based tend to see emotional life in personal terms alone. Crucially, psychotherapy helped me accept more emotional aspects of my experience that were too readily devalued within the intellectual and political cultures with which I identified. Alternative forms of psychotherapy created time and space for exploration of unresolved issues and helped to validate emotions and feelings as sources of knowledge.

For me there was also a link with feminism, which was liberating because it allowed for more equal communication within relationships. It recognized how people within a rationalist culture eagerto take what people say at face value were often false with each other and made little genuine contact. Feminism also helped me to honour truthfulness and honesty within intimate and sexual relationships so that I could bring more aspects of my experience into relationships. The early experiences of consciousness raising allowed me, as a man, to share fears and vulnerabilities that would otherwise remain hidden. I questioned a dominant culture that, in the early 1970s, still said that if boys cry this only proves that they are not "man enough". I learned to value emotions and feelings as I had learned to value ideas and language.[3]

Feminism was crucial in recognizing how the personal was political. It refused to separate reason from emotion. In this respect it was a crucial challenge to an Enlightenment vision of modernity. It served to acknowledge women's own sexual feelings and pleasures, which had been suppressed and denied within a patriarchal culture. It served to acknowledge the body and sexuality as part of a revised notion of personal identity. It implicitly challenged a dominant Christian tradition that had traditionally identified body and sexuality with the sins of the flesh.[4] According to this tradition, sexuality had to be curbed and controlled as part of an 'animal nature' and we could only aspire to 'become human' if we separated from bodies and sexualities. Sexuality was deemed to be a threat to Christian notions of purity and spirituality. For love to be 'pure' it had to be untainted by the body and sexuality. This made it difficult to fully accept Freud's revolutionary challenge to modernity, which was crucially to recognize sexuality as an expression of humanity.

For Freud it was possible for sexuality to be valued at the same time as it remained a phenomenon of mental life, for he was crucially concerned with the unconscious as a feature of mental life. It was left to Reich to fully work to reinstate the body in relation to emotional life. This was to unwittingly echo a Jewish challenge to an Enlightenment vision of modernity and suggests an unacknowledged connection between Judaism and feminism as critiques of a modernity that has largely been set within the secularized terms of a Protestant rationalist tradition within Christianity. Both Judaism and feminism, in their different ways, served to reinstate the body and sexuality as forms of knowledge, as ways of exploring different connections with the self. In the early second-wave feminism of the 1970s there was a stress on the universally shared experiences of women. This was validated in relation to men's control of women's bodies and sexualities, which crossed the boundaries of diverse cultures and was crucially linked to an exploration of men's violence in relation to women.

If feminism tended to stress what women shared in their subordination to men's power, it soon learned to listen to the different voices of women of colour. They insisted that racism gave them a different relationship with the family, which was not only a site of male dominance but was also a space of resistance against a racist culture. Feminism had to learn not to generalize from the experience of a particular white middle-class experience, at the same time learning how to affirm a subordination that women could share. Issues of rape and sexual harassment showed how different forms of male power operated in different cultural contexts. Postmodern feminism also raises questions of epistemology and ethics. An emphasis upon the ways that experience is provided through language could unwittingly make people assume that, for instance, there was no such thing as abuse or rape when it was not named as such. But this creates its own forms of moral insensitivity as it fails to name and identify women's sufferings of sexual abuse. The fact that sex was traditionally regarded as a woman's duty to her partner shows the level of denial and subordination that was expected from women within patriarchal relation-ships, which even sought to deprive them of a right to their own sexual pleasure.

Feminism diversified as it slowly learned to come to terms with difference. This meant questioning a universalism that was often implicit. There had been, in second-wave feminism, an attempt to assert the priority of a shared experience of sisterhood, but this had to give way to a recognition of the very different positions that women occupied. For some this meant that the very category of 'woman' became suspect as dreams of emancipation began to fade within postmodern theories.[5]

A younger generation of women no longer hoped for liberation but was ready to settle for shared opportunities with men within the public sphere as long as men were more ready to share childcare and domestic work. But a theoretical recognition of difference at the same time created a space to consider Jewish difference, and Jewish women and men began to explore the gender assumptions of their particular traditions. This meant recovering a sense of history and culture that, for many, had been forsaken in the search for assimilation into a dominant culture. The second generation, who had grown up in the shadow of the Shoah, began to ask their parents about where they came from and sought to break the silences that affected so many families.

Virtual Geographies

With the end of communist rule in Eastern Europe and the creation of independent states in the countries that used to be under the control of the Soviet empire, there was a new geography emerging in Europe. Europe was no longer radically divided and it seemed possible to rediscover connections that had long been denied. I knew that my mother had come from Vienna and my father had come from Warsaw, but Poland did not exist as a geographical space for me, a country with complex histories and traditions. Even though I knew that I could go there, it seemed far removed from my mental map of Europe. At some level I read and identified with events in Poland, especially as Solidarity formed itself as a political movement of resistance. But at a different level Poland remained part of an imaginary map for me. It was a place on a psychic map but it could not really be visited.

Somehow this was connected to a sense that there was also no time that existed before the war. I felt as if, at some level, time itself began with the end of the Second World War, which became the beginning of time as I could experience it. I felt a gap in my own experience as I could not reach back into the Holocaust. I knew the images too well and had often felt emotionally overwhelmed and drained by them but at some level, however much I was exposed to them, I could not really make them real to me. As a child I watched the early newsreels on television and I knew that the people on them were Jews and that my own family had perished in the Shoa. But I still do not feel I can 'come to terms' with these images, whatever that involves. At some level I shy away, fearing that whatever boundaries I have created for myself could simply be shattered. I have learned to tread carefully and talk very little about something I feel I still understand so little.

I was talking to a friend, Dennis Scott, about work that he does with his partner, Angelika Strixner, in Germany with people coming to terms with their ancestors. He described the difficulties many young Germans feel in connecting with ancestors, as if there is a hole represented by the war that is also difficult for them to penetrate.[6] Often their parents also refused to talk about what had happened during the war, as if it is a time that could be banished from existence. This can make it difficult for them to *ground* their experience, to feel that they have inherited traditions from their ancestors. In fact the very term 'ancestor' can cease to have any resonance or meaning because it suggests a relationship to the past that no longer seems to exist. Where the past might have existed, there is an absence. Denise talked of different ways he and Angelika had developed to work with these young Germans to help them face the hole and feel some connection to the past through it. This involves emotional work of great sensitivity. They think of the *hara,* an area at the base of the spine, as a space through which an ancestral flow can move. By maintaining a conscious connection with that aspect of the aura, they can begin to discover memories that have rested dormant.

For a time I had recognized a sense of envy in relation to talk of 'ancestors'. It made little sense to me because I had a sense of a physical gap that could not be crossed – the Shoah. I had known in general terms what had happened to my family but it was only in 1995 that my brother finally passed on to me a document signed in Paris in the early 1950s, which set down what had happened to my father's brothers, and their wives and children (see the Appendix). I remember walking along a beach in Jutland, on the western coast of Denmark in 1996, soon after I received this note. My tears gave way to a chant as I walked along the beach, mourning for those who had not been mourned. I could feel, possibly for the first time, the loss of individuals, of uncles, aunts and cousins whom I had never known. I felt their loss as individuals and experienced an intense sense of pain that I had not really allowed myself before. I recognized these uncles and cousins as people I could have known and I mourned their loss. I cried out to the heavens in a rage, for this was also part of my mourning. I felt their loss *as* individuals and this helped me experience the loss of others in the Jewish family.

I learned that one uncle had been killed in the Warsaw ghetto and that two others had died in Treblinka. Chaim, one of the uncles, had been able to hide in the Aryan part of Warsaw with his sisters in law and their children. I still do no know the names of the children or how many they were. The Nazis announced that, for a certain sum, they would allow Jews to escape to a neutral country. Chaim and his friends were ready to come out of hiding. Although they were hiding in separate places, they were in contact. But at the last moment Chaim's friend decided that he would not give himself up so he survived to tell what happened. They had given themselves up at the Hotel Polski only to be arrested, taken to the local prison and shot. [The Case of Hotel Polski by Abraham Shulman, New York Holocaust Library, 1982] The women and children, my aunts and cousins, were also shot. The Nazis had betrayed them. To us now it might seem incredible that they were ready to believe the Nazis in the first place after everything that had happened. But they did, and they perished as a consequence.

Having the document in my hand had made such a difference. It was not simply that I now had knowledge, whereas before I only had stories.

The materiality of the document somehow helped me feel the reality of what had happened. Somehow it had helped me deconstruct the 'six million', and begin to recognize that it comprises individuals and their suffering and loss. It is the overwhelming scale of the tragedy that can make it so difficult to comprehend, but at some level it makes it manageable and in this way we can protect ourselves against our own feelings. This has also made it harder for Jews to come to terms with what happened in the Shoah emotionally. There is a hardening process that can take place as people resolve through will and determination that nothing like this will ever be allowed to happen again. But this can also be part of a process in which we know intellectually what happened but we cannot really feel for ourselves the reality of the destruction of so many individual lives.

Our Jewish masculinities can feel threatened because we often learned as young boys growing up in the 1950s that the Jews 'went like lambs to the slaughter'. At some level we did not want to accept this. We often preferred to recover the acts of resistance and heroism and to retell the stories of the Warsaw ghetto uprising when, against all the odds, the Jewish resistance fighters held back the Nazi advance. But if they died with dignity, so did millions of others who found their own forms of spiritual resistance, who refused to give up their beliefs and values.

Resistance and 'Eradication'

Christianity had constructed itself around the symbol of a suffering Jesus dying on the cross, but it was always difficult for Christianity to recognize and honour its Jewish sources. Christian anti-Semitism had a crucial role in creating the conditions that allowed for the 'final solution' of the Jewish question. Since the interpretations of the Church fathers Christianity could not accept a Judaism that came to be identified as 'Carnal Israel' because of its acceptance of the body and sexuality as potentially integral to our spiritual existence. Rather the life that Judaism was also ready to recognize in the body and sexuality came to be identified with the work of the devil and Jews themselves were often demonized within Christian writings. Judaism was deemed to be blind and the synagogue came to be represented, for instance, in a statue outside Strasbourg Cathedral as a blind woman using a stick to find her way. She could not see the 'true' path that Christ alone supposedly represented and she was destined to wander, unable to find a home in the world. The Jews were supposedly responsible for the murder of Christ and therefore they deserved whatever punishments befell them. But at the same time they received a degree of protection within Catholic theology for they were supposed to be present at the Second Coming.[7]

We tend to think of Enlightenment modernity as a secular project, but in crucial respects it was established in the terms of a secularized Protestantism. Luther was fiercely anti-Semitic and once Jews refused to convert to the new religion he represented they were to be punished. Voltaire, who established the terms of an Enlightenment rationalism, was also anti-Semitic. Within the terms of an Enlightenment universalism Jews were expected to give up their Jewishness as part of the price of emancipation, to be treated as 'free and equal' citizens. If they were to remain as Jews it would be in the private sphere alone, where religion becomes a matter of individual perfection.

As far as Marx was concerned, Jews needed to be emancipated from their Jewishness if they were to become human beings in their own right. He saw the Jewish tradition in purely negative terms as a restriction on people being able to think for themselves and discover the means of their own self-realization through their creative labour. Emancipation within a liberal state would do little to challenge the terms of capitalist exploitation.[8]

It was Herder, in his critique of Kant, who was prepared to question the terms of an Enlightenment rationalism to recognize that it was through an engagement with a particular tradition, rather than through a separation from it, that people can sometimes find a meaningful vision of freedom that also allows them a sense of belonging. He was less prepared to set universalism against particularism, as if morality has to be exclusively a concern of the disembodied rational self.

But it was Kant's enlightenment vision that became dominant within modernity. Kant articulated a Christian disdain for the body and sexuality as aspects of an 'animal nature' that needed to be transcended if people were to find freedom and autonomy as moral agents. For Kant, a dominant masculinity could alone take its reason for granted and was thereby able to legislate what was good for others. As a dominant masculinity came to identify itself with an impersonal and universal notion of reason, it reframed the terms of a white, Eurocentric, male superiority. Kant learned from Rousseau that women were to be identified with their bodies and instinctual lives and so were deemed to be less moral because they were less able to live according to principles alone. This was an assumption shared by Freud who continued to think of ethics in largely rationalist terms, as a matter of disinterested principles, and so failed to appreciate *how* feelings could be separated from emotions and given a central place in our moral lives.

As Rousseau recognized, women's sexuality was deemed to be a threat to male reason, so that women needed to be controlled by men 'for their own good'. This meant that men alone could be independent and self-sufficient.[9] It was supposedly only through their relationship with men, through the institution of marriage, that women could secure an inner relationship with reason. It was through accepting their subordination in marriage that women could supposedly find freedom and autonomy. This established the gendered character of a liberal moral culture. Women constantly had to prove themselves to be rational, whereas men could somehow take it for granted. This meant that the nature of men's dependency was hidden, as was their power in gender relations. Within modernity women supposedly needed men in a way that men did not need women. Thus it was that women could not be complete and autonomous beings inn their own right because they were unduly influenced by their emotional and instinctual lives. To be emotional meant that you could not be rational, for reason was set in radical opposition to emotions as a defining feature of modernity.

An Enlightenment vision of modernity gave a secular form to a Christian disdain for the body and emotional life. Where spirit was to be 'pure' if it remained untainted by the sexual and the 'animal', so reason could be 'pure' if it was untouched by emotion and desire. This created a fear of women's emotions and feelings, of women's bodies and sexualities, which were deemed to be threat to dominant male identities. Women's sexualities and bodies needed to be controlled by men and men had to learn to keep women 'in their place'. This served to legitimate men's violence in relation to women, for women could not supposedly under-stand reason and so could only be expected to yield to force. The idea that men can slap their partners to 'bring them to their senses' is still an oppressive feature of gender relations. Men learn to take their rationality for granted and this becomes a mark of their superiority in relation to women. But this is also what makes emotions so threatening to men, at least emotions of sadness, loss and vulnerability, which are taken to be signs of weakness. For men to open to an accusation of 'weakness' is to bring their heterosexual masculinities into question. For men to admit to emotions means that they are 'feminine' because emotions are defined within a rationalist vision of modernity as 'feminine'.

Modernity is established within a framework that sets culture against nature, reason against emotion, mind against the body. It provides, particularly in Kant's writings, a secularized form for the disdain of emotions and feelings not only as 'feminine' but as linked to an 'animal' nature. To be human is to be rational, for reason is established as an independent faculty separated from nature. In this context modernity is not only a project of a dominant masculinity, as Francis Bacon had already recognized when he called the new science a 'masculine philosophy', but reason becomes the defining quality of a new humanism. We no longer think about the development of character as involving the education of emotional life, as might be familiar to Erasmus. Rather The scientific revolutions of the seventeenth century serve to legitimate the 'feminine' as a threat to knowledge, which has to be objective and impartial.[10]

In Kant's moral theory we have to eradicate emotions, feelings and desires positioned as forms of unreason and determination so that we can respond to the voice of reason alone. Morality is defined as a rationalist project in which is reason radically separated from nature. We have to 'rise above' our 'animal natures', for it is only as rational selves that we can be moral agents.

A dominant masculinity learns to control emotional life as a process of suppression. Men learn to fear the revelation of their natures, for this might threaten the images they have of themselves as rational selves. In this framework it is men alone who are fully 'human' and the fact that women are deemed to be 'closer to nature' means that they are 'less than human'. Sexuality and emotional life are not 'part of' what makes us 'human', rather they exist as threats to an existence as rational selves. They are to be disdained as part of an 'animal nature'. This is what creates the 'women's question', for within the terms of an Enlightenment vision of modernity their status as human beings is problematic. They cannot be complete in themselves, but for Kant they can only secure their 'humanity' through subordinating themselves to the guidance of a male reason. It is through their relationships with men that women can learn to exercise control over their 'animal natures'.

The French Revolution saw itself as offering a solution to the 'Jewish question', which had also marked Christian Europe. This is a theme which Marx explores in his essay 'On the Jewish Question', which I have discussed in *Recovering the Self*. He discerns different stages of emancipation. Seeing Jewish traditions as 'backward' he welcomes the emancipation of Jews from their Jewishness. He still shares the modernist vision that to be human is to be rational and that reason provides the central quality of a shared humanity. Differences of religion have no basis in reality and are artificial barriers to a recognition of a 'common humanity'. It is through reason, not through ritual and tradition, that we should guide our lives as rational selves. This was part of the democratic impulse of modernity. Marx goes on to question aspects of this rationalism through his recognition that it is by creative labour that people can grow and develop into themselves. Freedom of speech within orthodox

Marxism came to be less significant than the right to work. But within both liberalism and orthodox Marxism there is a disdain for tradition and cultures that are deemed, in Kantian terms, to be forms of unfreedom and determination.

As Simone Weil recognizes, modernity was associated with uprooted-ness. Within the dominant traditions of political theory it was difficult to value the diversity of traditions and cultures. This was part of Herder's critique of Kant, for he recognized the moral injuries people can do to themselves as they split from their cultural traditions.[11] This does not mean it is not important to develop a critical relationship to religious and cultural traditions that can be marked by a pervasive sexism and homophobia. However, this is different from dismissing religious and cultural traditions as forms of unreason that need to be 'left behind' as people explore their freedom as rational selves. This is part of a tension between tradition and modernity that needs to be carefully evaluated but at the same time we have to be careful not to identify the authority relations of religions with spiritual traditions. Herder questions Kant's rationalism and universalism and suggests that different cultures express their own values through different languages. Often people can only grow if they can also respect where they come from and the diverse traditions that they carry.

A central contradiction within modernity, given its democratic aspirations is the ease with which we treat others as 'less than human'. Unwilling to recognize bodies, sexualities and desires as expressions of a 'humanity' rather than as threats that come from an 'animal nature', we learn to project onto others what we are often unable to acknowledge in ourselves. This is a critical insight in Susan Griffin's *Pornography and Silence,* which allows her to recognize connections between sexism, 'racism', and anti-Semitism.[12]

As a rationalist tradition teaches us to suppress and eradicate aspects of an 'animal nature' that are deemed to be threats to a status as rational selves, so we learn to project these feelings onto 'others'. This is true of the witch burnings in early modern Europe, where women healers were deemed to be a particular threat. These gifts of healing were devalued and treated as the works of the devil. We also know from the terrors of the slave trade the ease with which people with African descent were treated as 'less than human'. Again we can acknowledge the workings of oppression but we have to be careful not to generalize about complex historical processes.

The Nazi project of the 'final solution' to the Jewish question also spoke in terms of eradication. Jews were likened to 'vermin' who were a threat to the health of the body politic. The contributions that Jews had made to German culture over a long period and the lives they sacrificed in the First World War did not save them. Jewish people were to gradually find themselves excluded and marginalized, unable to participate in professional and cultural life. This was a great shock, for generations of Jews had accepted the terms of assimilation offered by modernity, and they had learned to represent themselves as Germans of a mosaic faith. Moses Mendelssohn had sought to prove that Judaism could be cast as a 'rational' religion, and many Jews prided themselves in their modernity. They learned, as Sartre expresses it in *Anti-Semite and Jew,* to treat their Jewishness as incidental. They learned to think of themselves as instances of a universal quality of reason so that it was their rationality that provided for their humanity. Religion became a matter of individual belief. Jews had learned to participate as 'free and equal' citizens within the public realm. Their religion had become a private matter with little consequences for their primary identities as rational selves.

Towards the end of his life, Sartre learnt to think of Jewishness not simply as a projection of others, but as a tradition and culture that carried values and ethics of its own.[13] He helped to name the implicit anti-Semitism that was part of a tradition of Enlightenment liberalism. Jews were acceptable as 'free and equal' citizens as long as they learned to regulate and control signs of their Jewishness. They would be tolerated, but at some level they remain shamed. I have attempted to share aspects of an inner experience of this process, growing up in England in the 1950s as part of the second generation. I have stressed how I wanted to be 'like everyone else' and this meant automatically learning to curb expressions and mannerisms that might be identified as 'too Jewish'. This was the price that I was prepared to pay, even if it meant distancing myself from Jewish culture and traditions. But it was not a process of which I was very aware of at the time, for a liberal moral culture taught that I could only find freedom if I was prepared to separate from a 'backward' religious tradition. I adopted a double consciousness that allowed me to 'pass' in different settings. I had learned that I had everything to gain and nothing to lose, for it was only the unfreedoms and determinations that worked to compromise my individual freedom that were being left behind. It took time and experience to teach me otherwise. Visiting Poland was part of a process of education.

Notes

1. This notion of double-consciousness was invoked by the African American scholar and activist W.E. DuBois and it is a theme explored

in *The Souls of Black Folk* (New York, New American Library, 1969). Recently it has been taken up in Paul Gilroy in *Black Atlantic* (London, Verso, 1994). The concluding chapter explores connections between the black and Jewish experiences.

2. For a helpful introduction to alternative forms of psychotherapy and the social and political context in which they developed see, for instance, Sheila Ernst and Lucy Goodison, *In Our Own Hands* (London, The Women's Press, 1981) For more bodily related therapies specifically, see Ken Dychwald, *Bodymind* (London, Wildwood House, 1978).

3. To help place the development of feminism, especially in Britain, see Sheila Rowbotham, *Woman's Consiousness, Man's World* (Harmondsworth, Penguin, 1973) and her more recent *The Past is Before Us: Feminism in Action since the 1960s* (London, Pandora 1989). I have explored the diverse ways in which men responded to the women's movement in Victor J. Seidler, *Recreating Sexual Politics: Men, Feminism and Politics* (London, Routledge, 1991).

4. To explore the histories of sexuality within a Christian tradition, see Peter Brown, *The Body and Society: Men, Women and Sexual Renunciation in Early Christianity.* (London and Boston, Faber 1990).

5. The diverse ways in which feminisms relate to issues of difference are explored in Seyla Benhabib, *Situating the Self: Gender, Community and Postmodernism in Contemporary Ethics* (Cambridge, Polity !992); Sneja Gunew (ed.) *Feminist Knowledge: Critique and Construct* (London, Routledge, 1990) and Pauline Johnson *Feminism as Radical Humanism* (Boulder, Westview, 1994).

6. Some of the experiences in the groups organized by Dennis Scott and Angelika Strixner have been described in a paper, 'The transformation of the shadow and the spark of active awareness' to be published in the Jungian journal, *Harvest.*

7. A helpful discussion of some of the sources of Christian anti-Semitism is provided by Franklin Little, *The Crucifixion of the Jews* (New York, Harper & Row, 1975). See also Richard Libowitz (ed.) *Faith and Freedom: a Tribute to Franklin H. Littel* (Oxford, Pergamon Press, 1987).

8. Marx's relationship to Judaism and 'the Jewish question' as a touchstone for understanding his relationship to an Enlightenment vision of modernity is a theme I have explored further in *Recovering the Self: Morality and Social Theory.* (London, Routledge, 1994)

9. Rousseau's relationship to gender and the different education he feels appropriate for men and women is explored by Susan Moller Okin, *Women in Western Political Thought* (London, Virago, 1980).

10. The ways scientific revolutions of the seventeenth century served to legitimate the reordering of gender relations is a theme in B. Ehrenreich and D. English, *For Her Own Good* (London, Pluto Press, 1979); B. Farrington, *The Philosophy of Frances Bacon* (Liverpool, Liverpool University Press, 1964); Victor J. Seidler, *Unreasonable Men: Masculinity and Social Theory* (London, Routledge, 1994) and Brian Easlea, *Science and Sexual Oppression* (London, Weidenfeld & Nicholson, 1981).

11. The way in which Herder serves as a critique of Kant and the Enlightenment project is a central theme in Isaiah Berlin, *Vico and Herder: Two Studies in the History of Ideas* (New York, Random House, 1976).

12. Susan Griffin makes crucial connections between sexism, racism and anti-Semitism though she often relies too heavily upon her notion of the 'pornographic mind' in *Pornography and Silence* (London, The Women's Press, 1980).

13. The different influences upon Sartre and the shifts in his conception of Jewishness in his later writings are themes explored by Judith Friedlander, *Vilna on the Sein* (New Haven, Yale University Press, 1990).

2

Jewish Identities

'Poles' and 'Jews'

During the 1990 presidential elections in Poland, Lech Walesa said that Poles of Jewish origin should declare themselves. Adam Michnik, a founding member of Solidarity and prominent political activist for change, who feels entirely Polish and cares little about his Jewish origins, told Walesa how much he resented this appeal to old demons. He felt as though he 'had been spat in the face'. It showed the residual anti-Semitism that was to surface during the elections, and it confirms the old prejudice that true Poles are Catholics and the others are aliens who might be tolerated but are still less than true Poles.

My first visit to Poland was in 1988, when the political situation was still very unstable and the outcome uncertain. I was to attend an international conference on altruism that was to focus on Christian rescuers of Jews during the Second World War. I was struck by the continuing unease around Polish-Jewish identities.[1] The intensity of the national struggles and the history of partition had formed a close identification between Catholicism and Polish national identity. I felt some of the historical sources for the separation that had divided Jews from Poles.

As we drove from the new airport into town, in November 1997, we discussed plans for the trip. I was to give lectures in Warsaw and Krakow as a guest of the Polish Academy of Sciences. I was pleased to be invited back but it was only in the weeks before the trip that I really took in that I was returning to Poland. Anna had decided to come with and we were going to visit the towns where her father and mother came from. We had both felt tense and emotional before the visit, unsure about the arrangements we were making for our children, Daniel and Lily, especially as this was the first trip we were taking without them. There was a lot of fear in the weeks before the journey. I had a particularly intense dream in which I was in a conference that I was not feeling comfortable with. I was not sure that I wanted to be there. As I was leaving to find some space for myself a large black dog bit into my right hand. In the dream it had the whole of my hand in its mouth and I could begin to feel its teeth breaking through my skin. I decided that I would calm myself and I was able to still my fear and this helped to still the dog. I felt that I was somehow more in touch with myself and no longer panicked.

As we travelled into town I mentioned that Anna and I wanted to spend some time on the following day visiting some of the Jewish sites in Warsaw. There was an uneasy tension in the car and our host, Professor Rosner, said that there was nothing to see in Warsaw because everything had been destroyed. Only later I recognized the sensitivity so many Poles feel about Jewish visitors coming to Poland to see the remnants of Jewish life. They resent the idea of Poland being a massive Jewish cemetery and feel sad that people do not seem to want to see the rich traditions of Polish history and culture. Some of this was explained to me later was I was walking in the Jewish cemetery in Warsaw with Andrzej Leder, a post-doctoral student, who had driven us. His mother had been born in Paris and she had returned to Poland as the only surviving member of her Jewish family. His father had also returned as a communist after the war. It was only years later, on a visit to family in New York, that Andrzej began to ask questions about his Jewish identity for he knew almost nothing about it. His parents had suffered a purge in 1976 because of their Jewish backgrounds, though as Communist Party members their Jewishness meant very little to them though their friends had been supportive, their sense of betrayal helped them begin to talk more about their families' histories.

I had visited the cemetery before but it is a striking place and the only part of Jewish Warsaw to have survived intact, so I was anxious to visit it with Anna. As we walked around on a cold yet sunny afternoon we could feel the presence of a vibrant Jewish history. There are some beautiful inscriptions on the many gravestones and there was a sense of peace as we walked. Andrzej talked about his efforts to connect to his Jewish identity, but for many of his generation this was more a cultural than a religious issue. He asked me whether I could read 'Jewish', for he could barely recognize the Hebrew letters. I felt a sense of sadness as I recognized how communism had so successfully worked to obliterate Jewish memory and tradition. As Moses Hess recognized, in his challenge to Marx, it served to uproot Jews and it served to diminish Jewishness in their own eyes. They had come to see themselves through secular eyes, which within modernity were often Christian eyes.

In a piece on 'Poland's new Jewish question' written by Ian Buruma for the *New York Times,* Buruma meets Konstancy Gebert and Stanislaw Krajewski who had both been raised by Communist parents to whom Jewishness was merely an opiate for the people – not even worth mentioning among enlightened atheists. Then the 1968 campaign was unleashed against those who weren't 'real Poles,' whose loyalties supposedly lay elsewhere. Gebert remembers being expelled from his high school and beaten up in the streets. He realised that his parents had been wrong: Jewishness did matter, if not to them then certainly to the thugs who attacked him . . . Gebert wanted to find out more about Judaism, to give a negative stigma a more positive meaning . . . [he] . . . bought books of 19th-century Jewish literature in second-hand bookstores.

'The good thing about the anti-Semitic campaign', he says, 'is that the shops were suddenly full of discarded Jewish books' ('Poland's new Jewish question', *New York Times* magazine, 3 August 1997, p. 39).

His friend Krajewski suggested a reason for their passionate embrace of tradition that Ian Buruma finds disturbing. 'Krajewski said that the more he himself "lives as a Jew," the more he felt accepted by non-Jews. Once you come out, so to speak, people no longer feel that you are hiding something, that you are trying to pass as something that you are not.'

I find this disturbing because it underlines the common assumption that there should be a natural distinction between Poles and Jews. Even the Polish Jews I spoke to talked about 'Poles' when they meant gentiles. Now this might be a purely linguistic convention, but Rabbi Schudrick confirmed that Poles 'don't know how to deal with Jews who don't deny their roots, but are not interested, either' ('Poland's new Jewish question', *New York Times* magazine, 3 August 1997, p. 40).

It seems as if traditionally Poles have felt easier when Jews are visible and comfortably alien. With the close identification of Catholicism with the struggles for national identity, it was easy to feel that true Poles are Catholics. Jews might be tolerated as an alien minority and some educated professional Jews allowed to assimilate into urban cultures.[2]

The identification of Poles with Catholicism makes it difficult for Jews who want to recognize their own traditions and community whilst affirming their identities as Poles. This did not feel possible for an earlier pre-war generation. A choice had to be made between staying with the Jewish community as Jews or else assimilating, as many intellectuals and professionals chose to do, into a Polish identity. This did not mean conversion to Catholicism but it often meant being quiet about their Jewish ancestry. The question remains in the post-communist period as to whether one can be not just 'a Jew in Poland' but also a 'Polish Jew'. This is an issue that Ruta Spiewak, a university student whom Ian Buruma met, is dealing with. Her grandfather was the famous Jewish historian, Szymon Datner, and she has not had to rebel against parental atheism or

Communism so that she can take her Jewishness more lightly. She heard about Jewish history and customs from her grandmother but it was her mother who introduced her to Rabbi Schudrich's community in Warsaw.

Ruta joined a Jewish summer camp but she had reservations because she felt the American teachers were trying to teach young Poles how to be American Jews. Ian Buruma asks her what she meant.

> Too Orthodox and too showy. I know that Judaism involves music and dancing, but you don't have to make such a show of it. And they don't seem to understand that there was nothing here for 50 years. You cannot start off being so Orthodox. I can't. I never will be. Kosher food. The Sabbath. And, you know ... stuff with boys – they're as prudish as the Catholics. ['Poland's new Jewish question', *New York Times* magazine, 3 August 1997, p. 42]

As Ian Buruma goes on to report:

> Dwelling on the Holocaust is not for her, either. She is irritated by foreign Jews who come to Poland just to see the sites of the death camps.
>
> Ruta, like all the young Jews I met, rejects the idea of moving to Israel. She is Polish, she says. She learnt the same things at school as her friends. She is no different from them. The culture she knows best is Polish culture. Again, 'We, Polish Jews . . .,' the poem by Julian Tuwin, springs to mind. 'I am a Pole,' he writes, 'because it was in Poland that I was born and bred, that I grew up and learned; because it was in Poland that I was happy and unhappy; because from exile it is to Poland that I want to return, even though I were promised the joys of paradise elsewhere.' But he was also a Jew, baptised, as he put it, in the spilled blood of innocent martyrs. [p. 42]

Naming Identities

As I grew up in post-war England I wanted to discover a way of being both English and Jewish. Sometimes this produced a double-consciousness in which I learned to be 'English' at school, learning to conform to what was expected knowing that this was a path to safety. Being Jewish felt an unsafe identity for at some level we carried the insecurities and rejections that our parents felt as refugees. We came from a 'continental' background so that it was still difficult to think of ourselves as 'English Jews'. This might be an identity waiting to be assumed, but my generation felt uneasy about it. We felt more precarious in our public identities and often Jewishness became a private matter of family and synagogue. We did not talk about it openly at school because it threatened the aspiration to be 'like everyone else'. We wanted to become English and it certainly helped us to know that we were born in England, even if it was of 'foreign' parents. We could be 'English' in a way that they could not.

The liberal and democratic traditions in England opened a path for us to 'become' English whilst maintaining individual religious beliefs. Within an Enlightenment vision of modernity we were 'free and equal' within the public realm whereas religion became an issue of individual belief. It was no longer supposed to affect our rights as citizens, although we were aware that with foreign parents we would not be able to enter the Foreign Service. We were also aware of issues of loyalty and constantly struggled over issues of loyalty to Israel, as opposed to England, and what might we do in an imaginary situation of a war between the two countries. We wanted to feel that we would resolve this clearly in favour of England, but we also wanted to declare the possibility of multiple loyalties. We were part of a Jewish diaspora but we could feel uneasy with a diasporic consciousness because in the discourses of Zionism it suggested the ingathering of Jews who had been scattered with the destruction of the Second Temple. We were anxious to be able to establish our claims to be 'as English as everyone else'.[3]

The Holocaust marked a radical break in Jewish identities. For those who survived there was a deep sense of rejection from countries they had loved, identified with, and in which they had made their homes. This was particularly acute in families with Polish Jewish origins, for the Jews had lived in Poland continuously for a millennium. There was a terrible sense of bitterness at the lack of support many Jews felt with the Nazi occupation. They had experiences of Poles having named Jews to the Nazis and taking part in the persecution against them. People who had been their neighbours had taken over their homes and possessions. Of course there were also Poles who went to great efforts to rescue Jews and to support them at great risk to themselves. But this seemed to have been a small minority and Anna remembers being told as a young child how 'the Poles were worse than the Germans'. Her mother had returned to Sosnowiec after spending the war in a labour camp in the Czech Republic. She was warned that it was not safe and that she should leave Poland. There was also the brutal murder of surviving Jews in Kielce in 1946 that sent a shock through the community. The message was clear: Jews were not wanted in post-war Poland.

Ian Buruma mentions Plonsk, an average small town in Poland, which was fairly typical in that before 1939 more than half of its inhabitants were Jewish. At one point, Jews made up 80 per cent of the population and there had been Jews living in Plonsk since 1446. David Ben-Gurion, the first Prime Minister of Israel, was born there.

After 16 December 1942, when the last train left for Auschwitz, barely a handful came back. Now there is said to be one old lady left of Jewish origin, and she is a Catholic.

In most typical Polish towns, the Jews were not mourned. New people moved in after the war, as they did in Plonsk. Young people were barely aware there had ever been Jews living in their town. In Plonsk, not only was the 17th-century neo-classical synagogue destroyed (by Polish authorities, in 1956), every mark of Jewish existence was razed by the Germans – the cemetery, the ritual bathhouses, every house in the ghetto. The Gestapo headquarters, on the other hand, survived. It was taken over by the Polish Communist Party. ['Poland's new Jewish question', *New York Times* magazine, 3 August 1997, p. 34]

The recognition that 'In most typical Polish towns, the Jews were not mourned' shows the emotional work that is still to be done. The connections had been long and complex and the histories so long entwined that the parting was unbearable. Jews felt betrayed and unforgiving. The survivors were often forced to remake their lives in other lands and they often talked in bitter tones about Poland. Anna knew that her parents were Polish. They used to speak in Polish when they did not want her to understand something, so it gave the language a particular edge for her. But it was only in returning to Poland and watching how people related to each other, the food and the customs, that she began to realize how much what she thought of as 'Jewish' was in fact also 'Polish'. It was difficult for her to make the trip back to the towns where her parents came from. When we drove into Strzemieszyce, the town her father came from, we found that it was bigger than she expected. It had always been a joke in the family that it was too small to have its name on the map. We found our way to the cemetery only to find that Jews were not buried in the town. We were told to visit the registrar in his office to check the records. It was only after he looked up the births for 1918 that he told us that Jews were registered separately. He had wanted to help so he had gone through the motions. We could not see any signs of the Jewish life that existed before the war.

In the aftermath of the war Jews turned their back on Poland and on Lithuania for their experiences had been too painful to share. Unable to come to terms with what happened themselves, it was difficult to communicate openly with children. There was an uneasy silence and the repeated notion that 'the Poles were worse than the Germans'. The children were to be protected from these painful histories, but often they came to unconsciously carry the emotions with which their parents could not really come to terms. These towns became mythical spaces in an imaginary geography, rather than places that could be visited. In splitting from the past it was difficult to feel rooted in the present. But the tensions were palpable as children were rebuked 'what do you know about suffering?' Incidents were alluded too, for instance, of women being forced to walk naked in town squares, which an eight year old could not have possibly understood. There was also anger and rage at the injustice of it all that could be taken out on children, as if at some level there was resentment and jealousy of the lives the children were living. At one and the same time the children represented hope and everything was to be sacrificed for them, whilst at another parents had been robbed of their own adolescence and so often found it difficult to let their children grow into their independence.

I know that my father had come from Warsaw but in no sense did I think of myself as 'Polish'. When I first visited Poland I was surprised by the expectation people had that I should be able to speak Polish because this is where my father had come from. I was ready for this time, though I was surprised to realize that my father's name Jeleniewski was not a 'Jewish' name but a Polish aristocratic name that probably was taken on because of some nineteenth-century family connection. (Since my father died in 1951 I learnt very little about his life in Poland and a few years later when I was 12 I assumed the name of my step-father Leo Seidler so that the name Jeleniewski fell into the background of my life.) When I gave my lecture at the Polish Academy of Science I was introduced as someone with Polish ancestry and I had to clarify that my family was Jewish. It was strange to be invited back and, for some people, there was an edge of suspicion as if my name meant that 'I was not really English' so that they might not be getting an English lecturer after all.

As I prepared for the trip I looked up Suwalki with some excitement, knowing that this is where the family lived till the 1920s and their move to Warsaw. I found that there was a Jewish cemetery and, just as I was resolving to visit, I read on that it had been destroyed and all that was left was a memorial that was built out of some remnants of scattered grave stones.[4] The feeling of devastation was difficult to take. But I felt excited to discover, to the north west of Suwalki, a small town that was actually called Jeleniewski, which was probably the estate to which the family was somehow connected. I knew that one day I would have to make a visit there. This time the visit was short and it felt a priority to travel with Anna and to share this experience together. We would visit Warsaw, where my father was from, and then go on Krakow, where we could go on to visit the towns where her father and mother came from. Though Anna grew up in Brazil and I had grown up in England we both came from Jewish-Polish families. Her parents had been survivors, which gave her a very different experience. But we shared a sense that these towns our families came from were imaginary and that history somehow began for us after the War.

Growing up in different parts of the world, it was Israel that offered a new locus for Jewish identities. Israel represented the future, where Jews could somehow live as Jews in whatever ways they wanted. In the 1950s we learnt about the *kibbutz* as an egalitarian community and we were filled with stories of how the desert was to be turned into green pastures. It had not been an easy name to live with, although I had learnt to use the humour it provoked to my advantage when introducing myself in secondary school. Timing was never well organized and it turned out that my name change took place at the end of my first year at grammar school at Orange Hill. Having been Victor Jeleniewski I became Victor Seidler. I did not welcome the change and apparently had to have it explained to me by the court before I would accept it. They said it 'would make no difference', but of course it did. I learned the importance of naming.

Language and Shame

Somehow Yiddish became a language of shame for us. My grandmother spoke Yiddish, although her usual language was Viennese German. This was the language we grew up with, although we never really learned to speak it properly. The focus was on leaning English and being able to speak 'proper English' because this was the passport to Englishness and safety. It was as if a line was to be drawn under the war and that we were not to ask questions about it. As children we soon learned that we were expected to protect our parents who, we knew, 'had suffered more than enough'. In some ways we learned to parent them. When my father died and my mother was left with four children to support, we learned to grow up quickly. We became young adults who learnt to look out for each other. We did not really want to hear our parents speaking German because this was to draw attention to their difference as 'foreign' and so was a threat to our own acceptance. Rather, we could feel ashamed of their accents, of their continental manners. We took great joy in the cream cakes, but we also assumed that this was the way English families celebrated.[5]

As children we learned to turn our backs on Eastern Europe. The existence of the 'Iron Curtain', as it was called, made this even easier. It was as if Europe did not stretch East but had borders of its own. This might have been where our parents came from but it was not where we had come from. We did not want to think that we could have roots elsewhere because we desperately wanted to discover them in England. We did not learn to treasure the Yiddish culture of our parents, although there were a few times when we visited Yiddish theatre and my mother talked of a Yiddish actor she knew who was sometimes on television. We learned to look out for him. But there was a sense that Yiddish culture represented the past that was over. It could not illuminate the present but it was tainted with defeat and destruction. At some level it became a language of shame and we learned at school that it was somehow not a 'real' language in its own right.

Rather we learned to look towards the new state of Israel and Hebrew as the language of a new future. We were brought up to take Zionism for granted, for this was the way that Jewish identities were now to be constructed. We learned about the heroic deeds of the settlers and we gave our pocket money to buy trees that could be planted in new forests. We were proud of the achievements of this new state and the ways it had accepted refugees who would otherwise be bereft of a home. Israel became a 'Jewish home' and I remember vividly the intensity of feeling when I first visited it as a young teenager. It was striking to see it as a 'normal' country, in which there were Jews doing every possible job. It felt as if there was a place where we were no longer 'tolerated' and where we could feel a sense of belonging. It was only later that we learned to ask questions about the histories and rights of Palestinians and the possibility of sharing land and living in peace.

As teenagers we learned to think of Jewish identities in terms of the diaspora, with Israel at its core. We did not think about a Jewish-Polish diaspora, even though Jews had lived there for so many generations. We did not feel that we had historical roots in Poland for this was a place where we felt shamed and rejected. But this meant that the vital connections to a Yiddish history, culture and tradition were broken. Sadly a false opposition had grown up between Hebrew and Yiddish, between the future and the past, between strength and weakness. These were false choices, for it made it difficult to value our sensitivity and feeling as Jews as part of a process of coming to terms with the Shoah. To grow up in Anglo-Jewry in the 1950s was to grow up in a frozen community, which had not discovered ways of meaningfully coming to terms with the complex histories it gathered together. In some ways we learned not to think about the past, but to face Israel as the embodiment of a different, more heroic future.

This helped to produce its own tension within Jewish masculinities for we often learned that during the Shoah people had gone 'like lambs to the slaughter'. It was only later that we learned to emphasize resistance, particularly in relation to the Warsaw ghetto uprising. It was often difficult to validate forms of spiritual resistance, partly because there was such fear of weakness for a younger generation that wanted to think of strength in heroic terms alone. At some level it linked to anti-Semitic notions that can be found in Weininger and others, which identify Jewish men with the 'feminine' and so with weakness.[6] This can create a particular intensity in Jewish men who can feel a need to prove themselves to be 'man enough'. It can also make it difficult for them to accept their vulnerability without thinking that this is a threat to their male identities. Within a Zionist tradition, the notion of the Jewish labourer and soldier became the icons of masculinity, rather than the scholar who had provided an ideal in the *yeshivas* in Eastern Europe. The scholarly Jew was seen as unworldly and weak, unable to defend himself physically. He was no longer to be admired but to be disdained. With the reassertion of a Jewish fundamentalism, often deriving from the United States, we find the image of the religious settler on the West Bank prepared to defend his territory with a gun.[7]

The recovery of traditions of heroic masculinities tends to focus upon narratives in the Shoah that stress moments of resistance and rebellion. Often young people learn less about the cultural and spiritual traditions that were alive in Poland and Lithuania, as traditions to be respected and honoured. When we visited the ruins around the Warsaw ghetto area we met a group of young Israelis who were visiting the concentration camps as well as towns where Jews once lived. This was partly a lesson in what should not be allowed to happen again. It was an exercise in will and determination, to show that 'Hitler had not won' and that young Jews were alive to participate in 'a march of the living'. It is less clear whether the students learned to honour the religious and cultural traditions that once thrived in Poland or whether they see these traditions as having failed because they could not resist Nazi power. At some level it can be seen as a 'victory' of Hebrew in relation to Yiddish, of the new Israeli cultures when set against the religious and political cultures of the past.

This raises difficult issues about the place of the Holocaust in Jewish education and the place of the Holocaust in creating Jewish identities. We can remember for the future so that we learn to honour the sacrifices that were made as well as the different forms of resistance, but it goes against Jewish teaching to emphasize death rather than life. To cement Jewish identities through fear does not only make young people value their traditions, it can also push them away for we offer them few ways of working through their emotions and feelings. Rather, we unconsciously teach them a fear of vulnerability as a sign of a Jewish identity that is deemed to have somehow failed historically. Daniel was exposed to this kind of education at his Jewish school and it effectively put him off being Jewish completely for a while during his teenage years. He did not want to hear anything more about Jewish suffering or about Israel. There was too much tension and too many unresolved feelings that could not really be talked about openly.

In part this has also made it difficult to establish meaningful dialogue between Jews and Poles, for both communities feel that they have suffered horrendously at the hands of the Nazis.[8] Often they feel that the other is not ready to recognize their own pain. But it is also difficult for Christian Poles to recognize any complicity or to recognize ways that Christian anti-Semitism helped to foster negative images of Jews. For some, the Jews were finally getting their due, for they were still held responsible for the killing of Christ. These views still have to be radically rethought for it is not enough to simply moderate their emphasis. It becomes crucial to open up a meaningful dialogue between Catholics and Jews and there is some evidence that this is beginning to happen. Until recently, with the end of communist rule, very little specific recognition was given to Jewish suffering, even at Auschwitz. Strangely, although Jews were rarely allowed to think of themselves as Poles while they were alive, when they died they were identified as Polish citizens. They were not to be remembered as Jews and at Auschwitz, until very recently, there was only a single hut that was devoted specifically to the destruction of European Jewry. In my visit there in 1988 I was struck by the absence of reference to the Jews, as it if it had been a necessity to obliterate Jewish memory. It was only as Polish nationals that their deaths were to be recorded.

During the period of communist rule Auschwitz became a symbol of Polish resistance against fascism. It became a site of Polish suffering at the hands of the Nazis and a reminder of what the Soviet Union had liberated them from. But it also meant that Jewish history and culture became invisible in Poland during these years. It meant that people did not really have to deal emotionally with what happened to the Jews living in Poland for so long.[9] If it was to be mentioned it was to be subsumed under the generalized sufferings of the Polish nation. It was as if Jewish particularity could not be recognized. There was an obliteration of Jewish memory in Poland so that there was no need for mourning. It was as if the Jews had not really existed but were part of a virtual community. As long as a younger generation did not think to ask questions about the

Jewish population in their cities and towns, the silence would remain. But it would be a tangible silence and in some ways an unbearable one.

Notes

1. The discussions from the conference, which focused upon Christian rescue of Jews during the Nazi occupation of Poland, have been published as P. and S. Oliner (eds), *Embracing the Other* (New York, New York University Press, 1992).

2. Some illuminating historical background to the relationship between 'Jews' and 'Poles' is provided in Magdalena Opalski and Israel Bartal, *Poles and Jews: A Failed Brotherhood* (Hanover and London, Brandeis, University Press of New England, 1992). See also the collection edited by Chimen Abramsky, M. Jachimczyk, and A. Polonsky, *The Jews of Poland* (Oxford, OUP, 1986) and Norman Davis, *God's Playground: A History of Poland* (New York, 1984).

3. Some of these conflicts within post-war Jewish identities in England, Scotland, and Wales have been explored by Howard Cooper and Paul Morrison, *A Sense of Belonging* (London, Weidenfeld & Nicolson, 1994) This text grew out of a series of television programmes and draws upon a number of contemporary interviews. For some helpful historical context see David Cesarani (ed.), *The Making of Modern Anglo-Jewry* (Oxford, Blackwell, 1990).

4. It was only at the closing of 1998 while continuing to research that I came upon a report in The Polish Ministry of Information, *The German New Order in Poland* (Hutchinson & Co, London, 1993) that 'The Jews in the Suwalki district, near East Prussia, were expelled as early as October 1939, and driven over the Lithuanian border. Their plight became known to the world owing to the fact that it was sometime before they were admitted into Lithuania, and during that period they were obliged to camp out in no-man's-land' (*The Times,* 7 November 1939, p 231).

5. The experience of refugees in England and their visions of what they wanted for their children have been explored by Marion Berghahn, *Continental Britons: German–Jewish refugees from Nazi Germany* (Oxford, Berg, 1988).

6. Otto Weininger's *Sex and Character* (London, William Heinemann, 1906) was a crucial influence in early twentieth-century Vienna. It helped to position Jewishness in anti-Semitic discourses because it served to provide them with an intellectual basis though identifying Jewishness with the 'feminine' in contrast to a 'masculine' Kantian ethical tradition. Hitler was to identify Weininger as the only Jew who deserved to survive. But he knew that he had committed suicide.

7. Paul Breines has explored some of the tensions within Jewish masculinities, including the Jewish settlers on the West Bank in his *Tough Jews: Political Fantasies and the Moral Dilemma of American Jewry* (New York, Basic Books, 1990).

8. *The German New Order in Poland* brings together some critical documentation relating to the early years of the Nazi occupation of Poland. It serves to document the suffering of Poles as well as the suffering of Jews who were being forced into ghettos. The documentation considers the concentration camps but closes before the full realization of the extermination programme for European Jewry.

9. For historical documentation about the fate of European Jewry and the details of the organisation that went into the 'final solution' see Raul Hilberg, *The Destruction of the European Jews,* 3rd edition (New York, Holmes and Meier, 1985).

3

Memory and Mourning

Personal Mourning

We were staying at the Institute of Organic Chemistry Hotel in Warsaw. It was really part of the university. So many visitors had been brought to Poland through the transformation to market capitalism since the revolution of 1989 that it was difficult to find rooms. Caroline, a colleague from England, had one room and Anna and I shared a flat. It was sunny but as the sun went down it became extremely cold. We were not used to it but we made our way into town with the intention of checking out the building that we were to meet in the following day. As we passed across one of the main streets I realized that we were just a few yards away from the building that my father had worked in and been responsible for reconstructing just before the war. It was a moving experience just to stand in front of it and attempt to feel some kind of presence.

I walked through it to the open green courtyard in the back. There was a tree there. Somehow standing there helped me ground my experience in some way. I felt some kind of link. It was reassuring to know that this building existed, even if it had been rebuilt from ruins after the war. I felt like standing in silence for a while. It felt good to know that I was going to be working in the Polish Academy of Sciences, which was just round the corner. It meant that I could return to this spot. In making myself familiar with it, I felt I was somehow getting closer to my father.

Parts of the old city of Warsaw were wonderfully reconstructed from the plans that were found after the war. The city had been almost completely destroyed. So many Jews had died in the ghetto that covered almost a quarter of the city, and so many Poles died in the Warsaw uprising a year later. The Soviet army was over the river but it did not intercede on behalf of the Polish Free Army. It allowed the resistance to be murdered. They were never to be forgiven. This incident was etched in Polish memories. For many people it meant that the communist period was, in reality, a foreign occupation. It is only with the end of that rule that Poles speak of an independent Poland again and link it to the time between the wars.

So many Poles had been killed by the Germans that almost every family in the country had suffered some kind of loss. People were so taken up with their own mourning that it was difficult for them to mourn for the Jews. It was also too threatening, for it raised uncomfortable questions about what had happened and who was living in which house. Again it is striking how easy it is, in Poland, to slip into thinking about 'Poles' and 'Jews' as if they were somehow bound to have separate fates.

Buildings hold memories. Just being able to stand in front of a building that my father had worked in somehow helped me to connect to him, but also to connect to myself in a different way. It was not that I was discovering lost roots, as if I somehow 'belonged' here in a way that I did not belong somewhere else. But it is partly an issue of identity and belonging. It did help me recognize that my father was Polish as well as Jewish. I could recognize this in the way that some men looked and carried themselves. What was possibly most significant was that I could begin to feel that I had a history that went beyond the war. It was a family history of work, of joys, and of sadness, which stretched back into pre-war Poland. Even if I knew this intellectually, I had not been able to experience it emotionally. As I have said, I had never made much sense of talk about 'ancestors'. I had some idea of what this might mean for others, but I had no sense that it could have any meaning for myself.

At some level I felt that I had a memory that could stretch through the tragedies of the Shoah. I could begin to think of uncles and aunts and young cousins. I could begin to imagine them playing on the streets and even celebrating birthdays and Jewish festivals with each other.[1]

Even after the war the family was never very good at celebrating birthdays. We did not seem to have much of a collective sense of time. We had personal memories, but there were few family memories that were ever shared. When my father died of a heart condition in New York, in 1951, it was soon after he heard the fate of his family. The evidence was there in a legal document. Nobody had survived. How could he live knowing that he had survived but no one else in the family had? It was to break his heart. He died when he was away from home and for years I prayed that he would come back. I thought that if I was good he might return but he never did.

As he died away from home it has often been difficult for me to deal with space. It is easy for me to still feel that if someone leaves, that person could have died. I can feel that I can only trust those I have everyday contact with. It was difficult when a close friend, Paul, who used to live around the corner with his family, moved to north London. It was not so far away but it felt like a huge distance to me. I could have maintained telephone contact, but at some level it was as if he had died for me. I could not stand the separation and it took time to recognize the sources of estrangement.

At some level this connects to ways I learned to cope with my father's death. My mother had gone off to New York to be with him – they knew his condition was critical. We were left with our grandmother. I am not sure that we were ever really told about what was going on. My mother tells the story about how her mother had told her to come back from New York after he died on a Thursday with lots of toys and to wear a good dress and to pretend that 'nothing had happened'. As my mother tells the story, when she arrived home my older brother felt something was wrong and ran upstairs to his room. But I do not know that even he was told. It was as if there was a feeling that if it were not spoken about then at some level it might not have happened. As children we were thought not to be 'not capable' of understanding. This was a way that adults often protected themselves for they found it very difficult to communicate with us. We learned not to ask. We knew that our lives had changed for ever.

It took me years to mourn for my father. I had to go through a ritual burying of him in a residential psychodynamic group, in 1977, to help me realize, almost twenty years later, that he was dead. It was as if there was always a shadow of him around. It was if he had to be able to die before he could serve as some kind of guardian spirit. I had made a visit to the cemetary in Brooklyn. That had also helped me realize that he was dead. When I was still a student in 1967 it seemed possible to realize a plan that my mother had for years for him to be reburied in Israel. He always wanted to be buried in Israel and we managed to do this just weeks before the final date. After twenty years they would not have allowed the body to be dug up. The stone gave details of his death. The stone mentioned Suwalki for he was buried in a plot that was reserved for the Suwalki community. But it was still years before, when planning this trip to Poland in 1997, I would have the map in front of me and discover where it really was. It was still very much an imaginary space for me.

I had been in New York and I was able to organize his disinterment. I made contact with the remnants of the Suwalki Jewish community and a kindly survivor shared pre-war photographs that had been gathered in a special book of remembrance. I was present as they dug up the remains and placed them in a sack within a new wooden coffin. This helped me feel that he was dead. I sat with his body in a hanger in Kennedy airport and I could cry the tears I could never allow myself before. I cried and cried and cried. I was alone with his body and I felt that I could speak to him in this moment of privacy before the body was taken off on an El Al flight to Tel Aviv, where it was to be met by mother and my stepfather, Leo.

Things are beginning to change but in the 1950s it was thought that children should not be present at burials. Adults often wanted children to be left with 'happy memories' so they protected them from sad memories. This is an empiricist understanding of memory that has little recognition for fantasy and imagination. I think it can interrupt a process of mourning and, once interrupted, mourning can be difficult to resume. It can take years, as I know from my own experience. To feel ready to mourn is not a matter of will and determination. So many people died during the war that it was almost impossible to mourn them. I still feel that talk of 'six million' Jews is overwhelming. I do not know how to relate to it, although this can be painful to acknowledge for I can feel an obligation to remember every individual man, woman and child. Only in the last year have I been able to experience my own family's loss in personal and individual terms. I have begun to be able to mourn for them as individuals who have precious lives of their own. Years later I found myself standing in Warsaw and I could begin to reflect on their lives there.

Sharing Memories

It is easy to feel surrounded by shadows when you visit Poland. I know that it is wrong to treat Poland as if it were a vast Jewish cemetery, but it is crucial to also understand why so many concentration camps were built there.[2] Poland was near to the largest Jewish populations but it was also on a rail network that allowed Jews, gypsies, homosexuals and political prisoners to be brought by train from all parts of Europe. Hitler's plan for the 'final solution' was no less than the complete destruction of European Jewry. There was a museum, already planned for Prague, which would show the remains of a vanished civilization. Ritual items had been collected from different parts of Europe to be shown in the special galleries. There were supposed to be few survivors and the Nazi policies were to stretch back into the third generation, when a single Jewish grandparent could condemn you to be sent to an extermination camp.

In Poland, relatively few Jews survived and those who did were discouraged from returning. Polish Jews have children all over the world, but few live in Poland. I was struck, when I first visited Poland in 1988, for a conference on altruism and the rescue of Jews during the war, by the way in which young people in Krakow were anxious to learn about the lost Jewish communities. *Fiddler on the Roof* was to be their source and the children I stayed with watched with great interest. They were also pleased to meet me, a 'living' Jew. At Krakow the first exhibition of Jewish culture was also taking place. Sometimes this enthusiasm for things Jewish can be difficult to take, especially as it is organized by many people who are not Jewish themselves. They feel a strong affinity with the lost culture of Polish Jewry and they want to revive it, or at least keep its memory alive. Can this be a shared memory, a way of helping Poland come to terms with its past? Are there dangers that it romanticizes an absent past and makes it paradoxically unnecessary for people to come to terms with their painful histories?

For generations Poles and Jews had shared memories. They had lived through similar histories and been touched by similar tragedies. Even if the Jews had maintained a separate existence with their own authorities, they had lived in the same land and often shared the same schools. But it is difficult to know what happened to these shared memories after the war. For many people it must have been very difficult to come to terms with the loss. The Polish gentile population had suffered so much loss themselves at the hands of the Nazis. There were also collaborators. Events moved so quickly and with the establishment of communist rule there was a splitting with the past. Gentile Poles were encouraged to participate in this new historical project, even if many distrusted it as a form of Soviet rule. It encouraged a radical break with the past and so made it easier to forsake the memories of the past. It was the present and the future that supposedly mattered within this new socialist project, not the past. The painful events of the past could be put aside, at least for a while. For some it could feel as if the Jewish Poles, who were once their neighbours, could be forgotten, at least in public. Grief remained a private matter and people learned not to speak about the time before the war.

The long Polish history of the Jews was to be forgotten. People were to learn to live in the present as if they had never existed. Shared memories were denied. The young were the focus for a regenerated civil society and they were not to be told about the Jews that once lived in all these towns. There were very few Jewish people left to add their own memories or to tell their own stories. Where there was once shared memories there was now only a painful silence. As Anna and I were driving around Sosnowiec with our young Polish driver, looking for sites in a town that Anna's mother had lived in, he would stop to ask people where the Jewish cemetery was. He would mention that he had tourists in the car, as if to create a safe distance, although he was a caring and responsive man who really wanted Anna to be able to make connections with her past. People were helpful, sometimes a little too keen to help even when they had little to offer. We were sent in a number of circles around the town before we reached the closed gates of the cemetery. It was Saturday – the Jewish Sabbath – and the cemetery was closed. But we could look into it, peering at the gravestones as almost the only proof that Jews had once existed in this community.

We thought that we were going to find an impressive synagogue in the town. When Anna visited the synagogue in Warsaw she found herself talking Yiddish to the *shamas,* who helps to take care of the synagogue. They talked for a long time and he mentioned the synagogue and the name of the rabbi who had long served there. It was a name familiar to her because her mother had mentioned him. It was a link in memory, however tenuous. But he talked as if the synagogue still existed and so it became part of our search.

The people we asked did not seem to know it. It might have been destroyed or put to other purposes but it was clearly not part of the imagined geography of the town any longer. I imagined that in the pre-war years it would have been different and everyone would have at least been able to give rough directions for it. But it was no longer a memory. Sometimes there was a painful twitch at the edge of the eyes, but it was difficult to be sure. People wanted to feel welcoming, but somehow it was difficult to trust.[3]

Shadows

Visiting Warsaw, knowing that my father's family had lived and died there. made me very aware of the shadows. I sought some of them out. Warsaw had had such a Jewish presence before the war that it was difficult not to experience their absence. It is the power of absence that is so striking. As we visited the white marble monument on Umschlagplatz, the point at which Jews were taken onto wagons for the trip to Treblinka as the ghetto was systematically emptied, I felt the presence of shadows. I held my breath. I don't think that I breathed easily most of the time I was in Warsaw. I did not know how I would feel. I withdrew into myself for a moment watching the first names on the monument. I immediately caught sight of Uriel, one of the guardian angels in the Jewish Kabbalistic tradition, who was also inscribed on the wall. It is difficult not to look for first names you knew from the family to see if they were also there.

It is a simple and fitting monument. Jews had traditionally been known by their first names, then linked to the first names of their parents. So it did not feel as if the list of names was incomplete but at the same time it felt as if anyone could have been included in the transports. If I had been there, or Anna, we would have been included and our names were already there as if to remind us of a fate that was also, in some sense, ours.

It was a cold afternoon and the sun was setting. I discovered later that Anna had taken photographs of the first names of her family. Even if they had not been there, in some way, it was a memorial that could also include them. Even though they had survived, it was an experience that marked their lives forever. It also marked the children, for they were to carry the unacknowledged emotions of their parents. It was as if they had to struggle hard to find their own lives, for they were so closely entwined with the fates of their surviving parents.

There is something holy in a name. In the Kabbalah we learn of how the letters rise up to heaven. Letters together make up a name.[4] On these white marble slabs there were lists of first names that people carried. It could have felt incomplete because the 'surnames' were not mentioned, but it did not. The name by which you are called as a child has a particular personal echo of its own. You could image the souls ascending but you could also feel the terror that was in the earth. As men and women, girls, and boys gathered at this point to be taken in cattle trucks, you could imagine the terror. It was an uneasy place because of what had happened there, and no monument could do more than mark the spot of destruction. The shadows remain. The cries remain. There is also a fear that others did not seem to care.

As we walked away from the monument, Andrzej, a young Polish philosopher, told me that it had been Easter when the ghetto was being destroyed. Easter is traditionally a time of celebration in Poland. People still live with the pain of that juxtaposition and there is a Polish book entitled *Umschlagplatz* that records gentile Poles' responses to that terrible time. Many people continued to be aware of the shadows and could not put their memories aside. They could hear the heavy sounds of destruction. A few offered help and there are some small stone monuments marking the route from the central monument towards Umschlagplatz, which record the assistance of the Polish underground. But the help was limited and, for the most part, Jews were left to fight on their own. There is also a stone memorial to Janusz Korczak, who refused to leave the children he looked after in the orphanage. He insisted on going with them to their death. The orphans were not to be saved, for they provided the possibilities of Jewish continuity. The Nazis were determined to destroy Jewish memory in Poland.[5]

In *Shoah*, the documentary made by Claude Landzmann, he shows the continuing anti-Semitism within the Polish countryside. There is a suggestion that this is the way that people can justify to themselves what happened in the past. Put crudely, the Jews deserved whatever happened to them so you continue to have anti-Semitism even without many Jews. It remains a feature of Polish culture and shows the unease that still exists in relation to the past. The shadows are not only in the past but they inhabit the present. This is different from England, where we grew up knowing some of the survivors. We knew that terrible things had happened in the war and that Jews, along with gypsies and homosexuals, were selected out as particular targets. We also knew that this was to be the 'final solution' of the Jewish question. The Jews were to be 'eradicated'. But in Poland you have to deal with the absence of Jews in a way that is particularly striking. You might feel similar in Lithuania, the Czech Republic, Slovenia, Hungary and Romania, where there had also been very substantial Jewish populations that exist no more. The reassertion of anti-Semitism and xenophobia become ways of closing off painful memories from the past at the moment when they could emerge because of the collapse of communist rule and the ideologies sustaining it.

As I stood in front of the house my father had worked in and owned I was taken aback by the signs of anti-Semitic graffiti. There were hangmen with 'RAUS' written underneath. At a number of places on the building there were variations on the theme. I felt unwelcome. It was not what I expected. It was close to home. I felt fearful but I did not really want to feel afraid. You might have seen similar skinhead graffiti in different part of Europe, but it seemed to carry a particular significance here in Poland. It seemed to signal a determination not to face the painful histories of the past. Even though few Jews survived, they were still to be blamed for whatever might be going wrong in Poland. They were to get the message that they were not welcome here. Anna's mother had felt this when she returned to Sosnowiec after the war. She was warned not to return and that others had occupied the flats her family had lived in. It was as if there was a determination that the 'slate be wiped clean' and that Jewish memory would not be allowed to return. There was not to be mourning for the Jews who had perished. This was bound to affect the ways that Poland could come to terms with its own history and loss. This could also be part of the attraction for younger Poles discovering their Jewish connections, for it had come to have the attraction of something exotic – still almost forbidden fruit.

Before the war, at least a third of the population of Warsaw was Jewish. Jews were not regarded as a large minority but as a separate nation. This is how most Jews regarded themselves though about 10 per cent felt different and were keen to be assimilated into Polish culture. They were professionals, intellectuals and artists who identified with modernity and were ready to separate from what they deemed to be superstitious religious traditions. There was also a strong secular Jewish socialist tradition represented by the Bund, which organized its own Yiddish schools and saw Judaism in cultural terms. These Jews identified with Poland and were antagonistic towards Zionist aspirations. Their history was in Poland and this is where they were determined to remain. They also played an important part in the Jewish resistance movements. There was a complex and diverse community with competing strands. It was by no means united or homogenous. There was a large urban presence, which should not be identified with the *shtetl* culture that is often romanticized as the sole representation of pre-war Polish Jewry.

Ian Buruma reminds us that one of the most moving and contrary statements about being a Polish Jew was made in the prose poem 'We, Polish Jews . . .' by Julian Tuwin. Tuwin had always rejected a specifically Jewish identity before the war. He was living in New York. When he learned about the destruction of the Jews he identified, for the first time, with Jewish suffering. But he was still a Pole, too. As Buruma recognizes

> His poem is an answer to those for whom the phrase 'We, Polish Jews' remains a contradiction: 'Upon the arm bands which you wore in the ghetto the Star of David was painted. I believe in a future Poland in which that star of your armbands will become the highest order bestowed upon the bravest among Polish officers and soldiers.' ['Poland's new Jewish question', *New York Times* magazine, 3 August 1997, p. 37]

But is this dream any closer to being realized over half a century later, and what does it signify in relation to different communities in Poland coming to terms with their historical shadows.

Buruma shares how Jews and non-Jews alike constantly tell him that Polish anti-Semitism must not be misunderstood. As he has it, many Poles are 'like pre-war Europeans; anti-Semitism for them is almost casual, part of the language, not meant to be taken too seriously' (p. 44). But then he recounts a meeting with a smartly dressed businessman in his forties, who was well travelled but suddenly informed him that 'the Communists tried to enforce "a Jewish mentality" and that the Communists, like the Jews, were "intruders" in Poland' (p. 44). Perhaps he meant this casually, yet it was still shocking. You realize that anti-Semitism in Poland, is not immediately associated with its most extreme result : the Holocaust. The connections do not seem to be made, though to a visitor it is that catastrophe that is so hard to forget in Poland. There does not seem to be an awareness of the dangers of racism and anti-Semitism or any sense – widespread in Western Europe – that racism threatens democracy. Many Poles still associate communism with the relatively large numbers of Jews who served in its ranks. This can also be played on by the Catholic Church. Even if the Polish Pope had made efforts to mend the Church's fraught relations with the Jews, old prejudices die hard. Polish prelates on occasion still complain about conspiring Jews always picking on Poland, as happened when Carmelite nuns established a convent at Auschwitz in 1984.

It is striking that, even after all the horrors of the War, anti-Semitism in Poland is not taboo. As Gebert thinks about it 'Polish anti-Semitism is frightening to me not as a Jew but as a democrat.' As Joachim Russek tried to explain to us on our visit to the Jewish Cultural Centre of which he is a director, in Kazimierz, the old Jewish district in Krakow, it is a sign that after fifty years of communist rule a democratic culture will take time to establish itself. Only when Poland becomes an open democratic society can Polishness be a question of citizenship, not blood or religion. Then anti-Semitism might not simply be treated as a 'problem' for Jews but it will be recognized as a threat to the whole society. But this involves a radical transformation in notions of Polish citizenship, which has historically tied itself so closely to the Catholic Church. It is the Church that has also reasserted itself in recent post-communist times as a crucial power within civil society, making abortion illegal and contraception difficult to talk about openly. A Church that is confident that it, alone, is the bearer of truth makes it difficult genuinely to value pluralism in Polish society.

Many young Jews in Poland want to reconnect to their histories and traditions and they want to be able to pass them on to their children. But if these Jews are part of a revival in Jewish life, the sad truth is that nearly all of the community was destroyed. A revival in interest in Jewish culture within the wider population has to be welcomed and it might help the Jews of Poland to survive as a community. But it also matters that people no longer excuse racism and anti-Semitism or assume that it does not really matter because it reflects a small group of skinheads who lack parliamentary representation. As Gebert says 'When I see graffiti in Warsaw saying, "Gas the Jews!" I don't worry about the guy who did it. I worry about the fact that nobody particularly cares' ('Poland's new Jewish question', *New York Times* magazine, 3 August 1997, p. 44). When the only remaining synagogue in Warsaw, the Nozyk Synagogue, was firebombed and the front entrance scorched by fire, at least all the political parties, except those on the right, turned up for the protest demonstration. But the Catholic Church still only sent a message of sympathy.

Buruma reports how the relations between the old and new Polish Jews was complex, even antagonistic. The old were Yiddish-speaking survivors of a pre-war Poland whereas the new, young Polish Jews were Hebrew speakers, but also looking to make a Jewish life in Poland. The Yiddish-speaking survivors have become accustomed to being the last, lonely Polish Jews. As Buruma says:

> That broken shred of identity is all they had left. Marek Edelman, the only surviving leader of the Warsaw Ghetto uprising, once told Konstanty Gebert, the founding editor of *Midrasz:* 'You guys are a fraud, a literary fiction. The Jewish people are dead, and you have simply thought yourselves up, looking for originality and exoticism. You are not real.' ['Poland's new Jewish question', *New York Times* magazine, 3 August 1997, p. 38]

There is an investment, for the old survivor generation, in the notion that Poland, for the Jews, is dead. Many survivors feel this way. There is a feeling that the people who managed to survive have a right to live out their lives in Poland, but others should leave for Israel or another country. This is a strongly held sentiment in the survivor community. For them Poland, after all it has done and not done for the Jews, does not deserve to have Jews living there. The War saw the closing chapter of Jewish life in Poland.

But the new Jews feel different. They somehow want to keep Jewish memory alive in Poland. They want to live as Jews and they want to live as Poles. They want it to be possible, even if it has not been possible before, to live as Polish Jews. Somehow they want to be modern Polish Jews. For many it has been a long and painstaking task to connect to Jewish history and culture. In the long years of communism it was an absence, and it can still feel painful to recognize the distance they feel from Hebrew and Yiddish culture. For many, their Jewishness is something about which they still feel a little unsure, rather than something with which they were brought up.

Often these new Jews identify more with Jewish culture than with religion or spiritual traditions. At the same time they identify with Hebrew rather than with Yiddish. which might be associated with a Jewish separatism that they want to reject. Krajewski put the position most forcibly to Ian Buruma 'We want to live normal lives, do normal things. We hate the assumption that our life should be focused on living in a cemetery' ('Poland's new Jewish question', *New York Times* magazine, 3 August 1997, p. 39).

But many Jews who come to Poland from Western Europe and the United States to visit and to find signs of their families are often drawn to the cemeteries as the few remaining historical sites of Jewish life. The destruction has been so total that many cemeteries were also destroyed. They also visit the camps scattered outside the main cities, which are the sites of death. Somehow, like us, they want to feel that there was a past that stretched back past the days of destruction. But they do not expect to find signs of Jewish life and culture in present-day Poland. Although the revival of a cultural interest and the emergence of small communities of new Jews in search of their identities is a significant testimony to survival, it is not always welcomed. Nor do people want to know about the divisions within Jewish society and the movements that sustained different forms of Jewish life and culture. It can be enough to witness sights of a dead *shtetl* culture, even if they are romanticized such as in *Fiddler on the Roof.*

It has been hard to open up a conversation between different generations. The children of the second generation was often protected by their parents and told very little about their experience in the war. As it seems difficult for different generations of Jews to create a meaningful dialogue around the Shoah, it has not been easy to preserve Jewish memory in Europe. Traumatized by the destruction, it has been difficult to mourn and has been easy to feel emotionally overwhelmed by the scale of the loss. It has often felt easier for the younger generations to distance themselves from their own histories so that they could live more 'normal lives'. Sometimes the older generation kept heir experiences closely to themselves, not wanting to influence their children's lives. It is the silence that can be difficult, and the expectation that this is 'nothing to do with you' that can hurt. Survivors can say to their children 'you aren't interested' when they have never really sat down to explain. Sometimes there is more than an edge of bitterness and suppressed violence, as if these experiences are not to be talked about.

In the 1980s, some of the survivors, having spent their energies on making a living, felt that they now had time to share more of their experience. They wanted to tell their stories, but often not to their families – who needed to know the most. There had always been annual gatherings to remember the Warsaw ghetto uprising and a special day, Yom Hashoah, had been created within the progressive movements as a time to reflect upon the impact of the Shoah. It became an imperative to remember and young people were suddenly flooded with information that they could not always assimilate. There were academic conferences, most notably the vast 'Remembering for the Future' held first in Oxford from 10–13

July 1988 and a few years later in Berlin. The Holocaust was becoming an academic industry. But this did not always make it easier to resume a mourning process that had been cut off. Young Jews could still feel alone and unable to ask the questions that were troubling them, for now it was easy to feel that they should somehow already know.

I know the struggles that we had as a family, sharing our histories first with Daniel and then with Lily. We seemed to put off really talking about our different family histories with them. In a way, we were beginning to protect them, even if it was different from our parents. For Anna it was difficult because she was the daughter of survivors and she felt that they had told her so little. They wanted to put the experience behind them, but it created a tension in the family. We found a way in with a wonderful children's story – Lois Lower, *Number the Stars* (London, Harper Collins, 1994) – about the rescue of Danish Jews and then later reading Judith Kerr's book, *When Hitler Stole Pink Rabbit* (London, Harper Collins, 1971). These are wonderful books that share the authors' own experiences as children. Judith Kerr was a child of Jewish parents forced to seek exile first in Switzerland and later in England. It seemed as if it was easier to share these painful histories through the experience of children. Both of these books concerned the lives of children. Of course the children had already seen images on television and had to deal with things for themselves. We worried about what the correct age might be, but in the end we learned to respond to questions when they emerged. Sometimes we had such little grasp of our own histories that it was difficult to share them with our children. We each approached issues in our own way, but gradually found ways of speaking about different aspects of the Shoah.

Again, it was not simply a matter of sharing the horrors but also giving a sense of the culture and traditions that had been destroyed. This was something that we had to discover for ourselves. We had to explore our own relationship with Jewish spiritual traditions so that we could share our own joys as well as our grief. Children ask questions that parents can feel unprepared for. We had children when we were already a little older and in our different ways we were beginning to explore what Jewish history, culture and spiritual traditions meant to us. We were asking different questions from our parents for we lived very different kinds of lives and had quite different concerns. But it was still difficult to make the loss real to me because I had such little feeling for the Yiddish culture of my grandparents, my mother's family having moved from Poland to Austria where she was born, so little sense of the individuals and the hopes that were destroyed. This has become part of a slow process of change. The Jewish tradition has an evolving notion of *Teshuva*, which does not treat it as a moment of sudden conversion. Rather it recognizes the slow process through which we come to terms with our histories as well as ourselves. Visiting Poland with Anna was part of this process for me. It was also a crucial moment in our relationship.

Notes

1. To help 'coming to terms' with some of the experiences of the Shoah, it can be important to watch and listen to the documentary film, *Shoah*, by Claude Lanzmann, and also to read the text *Shoah* (Paris, Fayard, 1985), trans. A. Whitelaw and W. Byron (New York, Pantheon, 1985). It can also help to ready Elie Wiesel, *Night* (Harmondsworth, Penguin, 1986) and Andre Schwart-Bart, *The Last of the Just* (Harmondsworth, Penguin, 1974).
2. Some reflections on Poland as the site of the four Nazi extermination camps are offered by Gitta Sereni in *Into This Darkness,* where she shares her interviews with both survivors and perpetrators of Nazi terror.
3. In December 1998, a year after our return from Poland I learnt from reading *The German New Order in Poland*, that 'In Sosnowiec, the Germans set fire to three synagogues and arrested 250 Jews. Soon afterwards four German soldiers were found dead, and in reprisal twenty-five Poles and Jews were shot' (p. 247).
4. For an illuminating historical introduction to the Kaballah, the tradition of Jewish mysticism, see Gershom Scholem, *Major Trends in Jewish Mysticism* (New York, Schocken, 1941) and Gershom Scholem, *Origins of the Kabbalah* (Princeton, Princeton University Press, 1987). For a contemporary expression of this tradition see Adin Steinzalt, *Thirteen Petaled Rose* (New York, S. Aronson, 1995).
5. An account of the life and work of Janusz Korczak is given by Betty Jean Lifton in *The King of Children: A Biography of Janusz Korczak* (New York, Farrar, Straus & Giroux, 1988).

4

Fear and Belonging

Remnants

Growing up in the Jewish refugee community in north-west London we tended to assume that we were at the centre of our own world. Since we had not yet heard about the events in the Channel Islands from which Jews had been deported to death camps after the Nazi occupation, it seemed as if we were to be relatively 'safe' in England.[1] For years I did not really think of my parents as refugees, although I knew that my father had come from Poland and my mother from Vienna. We learned to focus upon the future and to turn our backs on the past. At the same time I personally had a very limited sense of future as my father had died when I was still very young. I have always found it difficult to plan for the future. I watch other people doing it, but it has little meaning to me. At some level the future feels too precarious and I defend myself against it.

My mother had been forced to leave the city she loved at short notice. She had to deal with a sense of rejection and she learned not to talk much about her family. We knew that her father had stayed to close up the business but never took the train to England. He was forced to retreat east, and ended up in the ghetto of Drohobitch. We think that he must have died in the concentration camp near Lublin.[2]

We never knew for certain what happened to him although my mother made strenuous efforts to find out after the war. There was little news. He had 'disappeared' like so many others. She did not really talk about him at all, and he remained for me 'my father's father' – somehow I still find it difficult to think or talk of him as 'my' grandfather. My mother's life had changed so radically because of the Nazi terror that it was difficult for her to believe in the future. She taught us to focus on the present and to find happiness there. She did not push us into occupations that we did not want to be in because there was a sense that life was potentially too short and precarious not to be lived. But she did want us to earn money, for this was a source of safety and respect in her eyes. But we all went our separate ways.

So many people in Anglo-Jewry seemed unaffected directly by the war, having emigrated to England earlier, that it seemed to hard to recognize that we were part of a remnant that had survived from Hitler's attempts at the destruction of European Jewry. It was difficult to bear the truth that he had come close to succeeding in his mission. To recognize this would have given us a special burden of responsibility as a survivor generation, but in our family, at least, this was not stressed, although we were constantly threatened with disinheritance if we thought to marry someone who was not Jewish. But we were still young and these threats did not seem to have much meaning at the time. My mother tells of the support that she received mainly from non-Jewish friends when my father died. She always remembered Mr Evans, a bank manager at Barclays, Mansion House, who was ready to put trust in her while others were telling her to sell the house we were living in and open up a sweet shop in Hackney. This was not for her, although ironically Anna and I did end up living in Hackney. We had moved into an area from which so many Jews were doing their best to escape. But these were different times and we were making different kinds of life choices for ourselves.

Many people in the second generation did feel a particular responsibility to redeem their parents' broken lives.[3] They felt they had to succeed in professions that their parents had been forced to leave behind to make a new life in England. I did not feel this particular pressure, although at some level I wanted to succeed to remain loyal to my father. When my mother remarried away from home in Israel when I was seven, I felt marginalized and excluded, and did not feel ready to accept my stepfather. He made efforts but I was not ready to respond. I felt that I owed it to my father to remain loyal and I think this was part of my difficulty with changing my name from Jeleniewski to Seidler during my first year at grammar school when we were officially adopted. When I eventually married Anna in 1977 I officially took back the name of Jeleniewski. I did not want to see the name obliterated along with everything else. But it was part of a long process, to both be able to feel that I could live my own life and achievements, rather than to feel that I was living in the shadow of my dead father. I could still feel that I was trying to prove myself to him, and that if I achieved enough he might somehow be persuaded to return from the dead. The boundaries between the living and the dead were never very sharp for me, because we lived with so many shadows in our family.

Psychotherapy was a great help in my healing process, assisting me to separate from my father and gradually helping me to live in my own light rather than in the shadow of my father. This feels like part of a continuing process. I gradually learned to feel nourished by my own achievements, rather than feel that I had to compulsively push on to the next project. I was gradually able to feel more joy and happiness in my relationships, more able to give and receive love.

Standing in front of the building in Warsaw, 57–59 Nowy Swiat Street helped me feel a more secure relationship with the past. It was not that I belonged here in a way that I did not feel I belonged somewhere else, but I could also somehow feel that I belonged here. It was also a moment tinged with fear as I became aware of the anti-Semitic daubing and it was difficult to feel that they were not in some way also directed at me. My father's family had lived in Poland for so long and my grandmother had come from Lublin before she moved to Vienna. Even Leo's mother had originally come from Warsaw. If I was to have any 'roots', they were surely here. I had also made roots elsewhere, and in many ways I felt strongly that I was 'English' as I had been born and educated here. I felt a love and identification with England, but visiting Warsaw this time also helped me to recognize that I also had roots elsewhere. I was part of a complex Jewish diaspora that had learned to belong between different spaces.

At some level it is easy to feel that whatever roots I have have in some ways been broken. As we grew up there was such uneasiness about Warsaw and Vienna, even if there was also some joy. It was too mixed up with pain for bridges to be sustained and for more cosmopolitan identities to be validated. Potentially we lived across different diasporas, but in the post-war period it seems easier to feel locked into a Jewish diaspora,[4] which had its locus in Israel, a place connected with a vision of future hopes, than to recognize that we were also remnants of a Jewish-Polish diaspora. Even though Jews had sustained a vibrant religious and cultural life for a millennium in Poland, it felt as if something had ended. This was a most violent destruction for the history had been so rich and complex.

Returning to Poland, however briefly, makes you aware of how complete the destruction of Polish Jewry was. Whatever the signs of cultural renewal with a younger generation of Polish speaking Jews, the sad reality was that so few survived and that this once-vibrant community was destroyed. This makes it difficult to honour this diasporic inheritance as one pole of identity, even though it remains crucial for restoring a sense of balance that the Jewish world find ways of coming to terms with its Eastern European cultural, political and spiritual sources. I think it has been a mistake to turn away from these cultural memories, devaluing Yiddish culture as a past culture of defeat to build a new Jewish identity, either through turning the Holocaust into a form of civil religion itself or else through an exclusive identification with Israel.

This is something that David Grossman the Israeli author of *See Under: Love* (London, Jonathan Cape, 1990) also seems to acknowledge, saying

> It is important to me that I write in Hebrew. I cannot forget that Israel is a miracle; that it took so many millions of Jews that were human dust and put them back together, to root them here amid so many difficulties – the wars, the lack of natural resources.
>
> All this makes the stain that is now spreading across Israeli society so much worse. Something went wrong here after the Six-Day War. The occupation tempted us to practise the most cruel and obtuse part of our psyche.

Grossman questioned the right-wing leadership and the self-destructive impulse that had intensified and 'which sees the solution to everything in taking a militant aggressive line. It is so stupid and short-sighted' (*The Jewish Chronicle*, 7 November 1997, p. 32). He seeks an alternative to this bludgeoning, macho approach that expressed a particular form of dominant masculinity. He seeks to recover what he refers to as 'the grace of childhood'. But it could also suggest the need to heal the self-rejection that identifies the traditional Jewish cultures in Eastern Europe as 'weak' and so as unsustainable. This is crucially the healing of a 'tough' masculinity that refuses to acknowledge its own vulnerability and so projects onto others, namely the Palestinians, qualities it is unable to accept in itself. This should have been one of the lessons of occupation – of the ways that it damages the occupier who takes up a stance of superiority. Possibly these are insights Grossman is seeking to work with in his engagement with Talmud study.[5]

As he puts it, 'I have come, more and more, to admire the mental freedom of the truly religious scholar. The daring to doubt, the flexibility, of the writers of the Talmud is something you don't see in today's religious establishment.' 'I know more about myself', he explains, 'when I read about Jacob and Rachel' and reading the Talmud 'connects me strongly to the infrastructure of Jewish language' (*Jewish Chronicle*, 7 November 1997, p. 32). It also links one to the spiritual traditions of Eastern Europe and enables a rebalancing to begin.

For Israelis, as for Jews generally, it is difficult to accept just how close Hitler came to the destruction of European Jewry. But it is unhelpful to conclude that the culture and traditions proved themselves inadequate to the historical situation so that a new beginning has been made necessary with Zionism. As Simone Weil recognized, this is to identify goodness with power and at some level to assume that the values of the powerful have been legitimated through their conquest. This was the path of Rome and it provided the model for Hitler himself to imitate. Rather than serving as a challenge to European culture, he was living out the ideals of empire that he had learned at school and that we unwittingly continue to teach our children.[6] This helps her situate fascism not as an aberration but as an historical phenomenon that has to be thought in terms of the history of the West. It is crucial to her that we are perpetuating, rather than questioning, Western conceptions of power and greatness as we teach children to identify with Caesar. Rather than, as Adorno encourages us, thinking in ways that would make fascism impossible, we are perpetuating the very traditions that made Hitler possible. Paradoxically, it is a lesson that is particularly meaningful for the Jewish experience, for it has also served to devalue Eastern European culture in the eyes of those who survive. It has meant that Yiddish has been rejected by many as a language of shame.

It remains crucial to question this identification, so central in the history of the West, between power and greatness. We assume, within a Western culture still shaped by Roman aspirations towards power, that whatever is of value is somehow sustained in those who have historically succeeded. This identification still haunts Hegel's vision of the dialectic. We assume that whatever was of value in the past is somehow preserved in the present. But, as Walter Benjamin also recognized, goodness is often defeated rather than sustained and the values we should honour in the past only exist as traces.[7] We should sometimes invoke the wisdom of the past as a critique and challenge to the present. We should question the notion that history is progressive and the assumption that with history comes the realization of freedom and equality. Zionism became caught up in this modernist progressive vision that made it difficult to honour its diverse cultural and spiritual roots in Poland and Eastern Europe. It became difficult to know what to value in the traditions of the past, and easier to think that Jewry needed a new beginning if it was to survive. In its own ways this has fed forms of Jewish fundamentalism, for when people have returned to past traditions they have often done so uncritically. They have failed to appreciate, as Grossman recognizes 'the mental freedom of the truly religious scholar'. This is also what allows him to say that 'There is something very secular about really religious people' (*Jewish Chronicle,* 7 November 1997).

Displacement

Families that came to England in the years before the war often felt an immense sense of gratitude. So few had been allowed to come, but those who were fortunate enough to make it rarely complained. However, they had not really chosen to 'become English'; rather they had been forced to leave the countries they often loved. They had been displaced and it was often difficult to find themselves in these new lands. They wanted their children to belong, but often they were not allowed to belong themselves. Leo's (my step-father's) sister, Hermie, who also escaped from Germany just before the outbreak of war, told of how she was in a shop, having been in England for over fifty years and a shopkeeper asked her where she came from. She joked that after all these years she is still a 'bloody foreigner'. It is possible to be tolerated in England, but it is difficult to be accepted as 'one of us'. But things have changed as England has become more of a multicultural society and there is less emphasis upon assimilation into a dominant culture. There is more space to be different.

Having also turned their backs on Poland, it can be difficult for the second generation to recognize just how Polish their parents were. Things that we learnt to think of as 'Jewish' turn out to be Polish. Anna felt a strange familiarity when she was walking around the streets of Warsaw. She felt that she could recognize her parents' friends in many people she met. The way they carried their bodies and the passion they showed in their speech were all strangely familiar to her. Having become accustomed to controlling my expressions in an English culture that still took pride in the stiff upper lip, it was a great relief to watch the passion and the emotional expressiveness of the Poles. This was also true of the food, which had tastes that took me back to childhood. This was the way that food used to taste as I was growing up. The sense that no meal was complete if it did not start with soup was also something Anna had grown up to take for granted within her family.

So visiting Poland forces you to rethink what is 'Jewish' and what is 'Polish', and to recognize that they cannot be clearly demarcated. The mutual influences were strong and if the cultures remained separate, they had learned deeply from each other. You could no longer disentangle the threads or claim ownership. Of course there were crucial differences between the urban cultures and the *shtetl* communities. As you learn to cross boundaries between 'Polish' and 'Jewish', you learn how close they had become to each other, even if religious practices remained separate.

Jewish people have often been forced to move between different places. They have become accustomed, in the twentieth century, to having their families scattered throughout the globe. They have learned to keep contact across space, but sometimes this can be difficult. Not many members of our family survived, so it was easy to experience space as threatening. This links to a difficulty I can have in sustaining relationships, experiencing life as if it were a series of discrete moments. I have had to learn patiently a trust in life that others might have taken for granted for it can feel difficult to trust that others can really be there for me. Since childhood I learned to rely upon myself and I found it hard to accept the continuity of time and relationship. Ever since my father died when I was still young, it was difficult to trust in the future. This exacerbated tendencies that were already embodied in the family.

My father and mother learned to make their home in England. They wanted to belong but it was not always clear the extent to which they could, or would be allowed to belong. I carried an unconscious fear that it was dangerous to care too much for my surroundings, for I would never know when I would have to move on. Spaces often felt unstable and I constantly had to be ready to move on. I still find it difficult to put time and attention into physical surroundings, to make the spaces I inhabit beautiful. It seems to have something to do with the always temporary quality of existence. Somehow having children helped to ground my experience and proved to be a welcome sense of release. I found it easier to write, although I had much less time. I was less concerned for perfection and more ready to accept things as they were. Children helped me nurture my creativity. They also offer an unconditional love, of you are ready to take it in. Receiving love was something that I often found difficult to accept in my relationships. It could feel easier to accept with children and they helped me accept that I could both receive and give love.

In our families there was often an unasked question that would not go away: 'why had they survived when so many had perished?' This was not a question children were allowed to ask for themselves. As children we often carried the names of our dead relatives. This was a way of continuing the lives they had lost but it was also to provide a sense of continuity, which I have often found difficult to feel. But some families felt that the war had cost them too much and they wanted to distance themselves from their Jewishness, refusing to really share their experience with their children. Coleen Guray, a participant in a Berlin psychodrama group for the second generation, had parents who distanced themselves from the Holocaust by emigrating to Australia in the 1950s and speaking little about their past. 'My parents' experience was like a vacuum', she said. 'I came to realise that there was a connection between this and my inability to feel rage, anger and grief.' She describes her group experience dramatizing family histories, taking on the roles of the different characters involved, as 'very healing'. She said: 'It was an encounter that started politely and full of avoidance. When pain, anger, rage and bewilderment emerged on both sides, we heard each other out and stayed in the relationship' (*Jewish Chronicle,* 7 November 1997, p. 5). Another group member Ms Weissberg-Bob wanted to take part in the class to disentangle herself from the past and learn about her identity, 'independent of (her) family's history', as she put it. She could sense her parents' grief, but this was something she 'could not get in touch with' (*Jewish Chronicle,* 7 November 1997, p. 5).

Sometimes people in the second generation can become aware of feeling that they do not seem to belong to the situations they are living in. Their emotions can feel inappropriate, as if they belong in a different context. I can feel that it is quite inappropriate to feel so insecure at work, expecting a knock on the door at any moment, as if I was back in Nazi-occupied Poland. My emotions can feel displaced, but it can still be useful to acknowledge them rather than deny them. In linking into my dreams and watching some of the fears emerge I can get some grip of what is beginning to emerge for me. A friend has a relationship with a woman whose parents are survivors. He can find it difficult to acknowledge her insecurities. He can unwittingly feed them by taking an objective position and refusing to engage with her directly. He is aware that his second wife has a difficult relationship with his daughter from his first marriage. He thinks that they should work on it together, as if it has little to do with him. But when he talks to his daughter he realizes that her emotions are directed more at him, at the ways she felt neglected when the marriage broke up and she was only nine. He can recognize that he did not respond well to his daughter at the time, possibly because, in his mind, she was unconsciously identified with his former wife. But rather than engage with his relationships directly, he positions himself in a slightly detached and superior position, familiar to a particular kind of Jewish masculinity.

This is another example of displacement. Rather than engage directly in relationships, Jewish men, from diverse backgrounds, often take on a detached position from which it is easier to legislate for others. Rather than engage more personally themselves, they can experience this as too risky, too threatening to their male identities. Having to learn to interpret what was expected of them from a dominant culture and unsure of their own instinctual responses, they can often be guarded. They develop a particular kind of sensitivity to others and can work out what is going on in relationships, but can find it difficult to engage more directly. This is not only an issue for Jewish men but it can be highlighted within marginalized groups who feel they have to conform if they want to be accepted by the dominant culture. There is an added pressure for Jewish men, as with Asian men, if their masculinities have been identified as 'feminine' within the dominant culture, for they have to prove that they are 'man enough'. As they become aware of the conditional character of masculinities otherwise taken for granted as given by nature, Jewish men have been involved in disproportionate numbers in the diverse men's movements.[8]

Journeys

Anna and I got up at 6 a.m. in Warsaw to make sure that we would make the 7.00 a.m. train to Krakow. We left Warsaw in a hurry. We had the train journey to prepare for what was coming next. When I was last in Poland, in 1988, Krakow had been on the route for a visit to Auschwitz, but Anna was clear that she did not want to make the visit this time. We wanted to search out the towns where her parents lived. We knew that this would be enough of an emotional experience. We wanted to focus upon where people lived, rather than where so many perished. But at the same time it is impossible not to feel as you move towards the beautiful city of Krakow that you are also moving towards Auschwitz. It is the proximity of such beauty and such destruction that is difficult to take. For Jewish people it can sometimes bring up feelings of fear just to be on trains.

As we were settling in the compartment, a man asked where we were from. Anna said that she lived in London but that she was from Brazil. It turned out that this man, named Adam and his sister Eve, had just come from Brazil two days earlier. They had grown up in Brazil ever since his high-ranking father, who had been a Polish military attaché, had been purged in 1956. They had come back to Poland for the seventieth birthday of their uncle and were going to spend a couple of days in the mountains, near Zacopane. These were the only surviving family as both their parents had died in Brazil. There was a strong feeling between them all, and it reminded me of the strength of family. But it also turned out that Adam not only knew Anna's cousin, Leo, in Rio but had also been a partner of his in a travel business. It seemed incredible to make the connection and to be reminded of family in this way. Before the trip, different parts of Anna's family had connected with her quite out of the blue as if giving their different blessings to the trip. Her cousins, Ruth and Martin, who now live in Toronto, suddenly passed through London for the first time in 15 years. Her cousin Mendel came and was able to give her the name of the Polish town where their fathers had grown up together. Then another cousin, this time from her mother's side, called from Israel to talk to her and give her news of the family.

The different fragments of Anna's family had somehow come together to express their support for the trip she was making. She was the first person in her family who was making the trip to see where her parents had come from. It was as if she was somehow making it for the whole family. They were travelling with her in spirit and were doing their best to wish her well. Everyone knew it would be difficult and that it would mean confronting a painful history. For years it had felt easier to put this history aside, to live almost as if it had never really happened, for this was the only way to feel 'normal', to feel 'like everyone else'. Sometimes if felt safer to leave history behind. It had to do with our parents but not with us. We could live lives of our own. It took time for us to recognize our different shadows as children of survivors and refugees. At some level we often did not want to know where we had come from, for we could feel that our lives had been made precarious enough, that it had been hard enough to separate from parents, to live lives of our own. But at another level we could come to feel that we had to face the shadows, if we were to discover more inner freedom for ourselves.

Meeting Adam and Eve in this way, and being able to speak Portuguese, linked Anna to different roots she had also established. It gave her strength and she became terribly alive in the conversation. It gave her the strength that she needed to take the next step, which was to arrange the visit to the towns her parents had lived in. They had told her very little, and the silence was painful, especially now they had both died. She could not ask the questions she now had, even if she wanted too. She had to do this on her own. But she could feel that there was an unspoken guidance, for visiting these different towns was also a way of connecting to them in a different way. As we arrived in Krakow another Adam met us. He was an old friend who teaches at the Jagellonian University in Krakow and my close friend Larry and I had visited him on our trip in 1988. We had stayed with his family and been very warmly received by his wife Margaret, and their three daughters. He had also made the journey to Auschwitz with us. It had been a difficult and moving experience to walk around Auschwitz and Birkenau. It created a bond that lasted through time. Adam met us with a welcoming smile and it was wonderful to be able to meet an old Polish friend who was keen to share his excitement about Krakow with us. He had organized the seminar that I was to give at the university.

Later in the afternoon we walked through Krakow to the old Jewish section of Kazimierz. It was already getting dark and we had an appointment with the director of the Centre for Jewish Culture, Joachim Russek. He is a very alert man who never seems to break from one activity to the next. He helped us organize a driver for our visit to Sosnowiec the following day. He gradually relaxed as we had a conversation over tea. We talked a little about the centre and how it conceived its role. It is a beautiful building, which has been expensively replenished with American money, but it can also feel a little strange. Its work mainly seems concerned with the education of Poles, as well as supporting visiting Jews as they come through. Out of the blue, as we were having some tea, he asked us whether we had heard of the death of Isaiah Berlin (who had just died). I was shocked. I had maintained intermittent contact with him ever since I was an undergraduate student at Oxford. In the early 1960s I had attended all the lectures and seminars he gave whilst I was there.[9] At some level I identified with him as one of the very few teachers I knew who identified with his Jewishness, although he rarely spoke about it in his teaching. But his concern with Herder was to do with issues of identity and belonging that at some level reflected his own Zionism. Berlin questioned the rationalism of an Enlightenment vision of modernity and the Kant's vision of the rational self that underpinned this.

Years later, I questioned him further on some of these themes as I was struggling to come to terms with my own Jewish identity. He was very identified with English culture and tradition and did not share the same feelings I often experienced. He seemed as ease with himself and could be very caring and even loving. He was drawn to the counter-Enlightenment thinkers because they recognized a relationship between language and culture and were suspicious of the universalism that informed Kant's thinking. They recognized the moral damage that can take place when you force people to speak in a language other than their own. Herder questioned the dominance of French and Latin and the difficulties this created for Germans trying to articulate their own experience in culture. He was also sympathetic to the fate of the Jewish people. He recognized the gifts that different cultures have to bring and so appreciated how humanity itself is impoverished when a culture dies.[10]

Walking around the streets of Kazimierz, feeling shocked at the news of Berlin's death, we managed to get the caretaker to let us in to the Temple Synagogue. We had missed the Friday evening prayers but we could spend some time slowly taking in this deserted building and its painted ceiling and windows. It was being restored but we could still sense some of its former glory. We could feel the presence of shadows, of all the prayers that had been said, the fears and the yearnings. I could say some of the Kaddish for Isaiah in a quiet corner of this empty synagogue. It was difficult not to feel a terrible sadness, for the building was here but the people were absent. It was as if we could hear their prayers and we wanted to hear their souls sing. The reality of the destruction was tangible as we walked through these deserted streets looking for the smallest signs of a Jewish life that had existed here. There are some beautiful synagogues that have been restored. The area still remained dilapidated but there were pockets of renewal that were not here when I visited in 1988.

Sounds of Silence

We returned to Kazimierz the following afternoon after we had found our way to Strzemieszyce and Sosnowiec. It had been disappointing to find the gates of the cemetery closed, but at least it seemed to be intact. We felt grateful for the smallest mercies and we searched for the smallest signs. It was still late afternoon and we both felt very emotionally drained. It had been a difficult experience for Anna and I think she was grateful to be back in Krakow. As we walked around the streets we could see the Jewish cafes, Jewish bookshops and Jewish restaurants that we had not seen the evening before. There was a Jewish cultural scene that had developed over the last few years, partly to cope with visitors but also sustained by a revival of interest in the non-Jewish population. Sometimes this felt a little difficult to take – Jewish culture without the Jews. But it is also moving to hear of the Jewish cultural festivals that have been organized in Kazimierz since 1988. I remember visiting a major exhibition of Polish-Jewish art in the main gallery when I was here last. This was to prove the beginning of a Jewish cultural revival that can only be welcomed.

Janusz Makuch, who is not Jewish himself and knew nothing about Jews when he was a child, has been driven by a sense of mission to revive something that had been pronounced dead. Ian Buruma asks him what drives him and again it seems to come back to the question of identity. He quotes him saying

> Young Poles are looking for their identity. We can't live in a vacuum. We have to ask ourselves who we are and where we come from. Jews lived here for a thousand years and contributed so much to Polish culture. I know that we are living in the world's largest cemetery. But when I see five or six

thousand people dancing the hora on the last day of the festival, Kazimierz becomes a magic place – and I feel the presence of the people who died here.

He might well be right. Dancing, for the Chasidim, was a way of coming close to G-d and expressing their love for G-d. The voice was brought into relation with the body and, through the sense of balance, a deeper connection could sometimes be established with the self.

Ian Buruma acknowledges that the language is sentimental but realizes that the context explains a great deal. Buruma comments that, with the destruction of so many people at the hands of the Nazis being followed by a communist rule that killed so many Polish intellectuals and tried to kill Polish patriotism and spiritual life

> Poland was culturally and spiritually gutted, and the post-communist void is rapidly being filled with the tawdriest products of Western popular culture: porno videos from Germany, techno music from England, action movies and MTV from the United States. No wonder the old, vanished world of Jewish seers and cantors and poets and sages seems like Atlantis. ['Poland's new Jewish question', *New York Times* magazine, 3 August 1997, p. 41]

As Janusz Makuch had admitted, it was a professor who had written a history of the Jews in Poland who had 'opened the gate for me to the Jewish world. For me it was like discovering Atlantis' ('Poland's new Jewish question', *New York Times* magazine, 3 August 1997, p. 41).

If these traditions have a special meaning for Jews, they can also provide wisdom and understanding for young gentile Poles, who can hear the sounds and listen to the music that was part of the larger Polish/Jewish culture for a millennium. It is to be welcomed for it respects Jewish memory and seeks to learn from it. This was part of the prophetic dreams of Judaism. The Jewish teachings were to be eventually recognized as universal teachings for the world, for particularity was not to be set in opposition to universalism within the Jewish tradition. A Jewish cultural revival helps to prevent the eradication of Jewish memory and the painful silence that you meet when you visit such towns as Sosnowiec. The older generation can remember their Jewish neighbours and the houses have their own memories that cannot be locked away. But philo-Semitism can itself be a denial unless it leads on to a questioning of Christian anti-Semitism and a recognition of the sometimes difficult relations between Jews and Catholics within Polish history. What is crucial is the way that these histories are being taught in Polish and in Jewish schools today.

With the reassertion of the power of the Catholic Church in Poland also filling the vacuum within post-communist Poland, it becomes crucial to rethink historical relations between Catholics and Jews. At a three-day Vatican conference on anti-Jewish strains in Christianity in late October, 1997, Pope John Paul II acknowledged that longstanding anti-Jewish prejudice had led to the passivity shown by many Christians when faced with the Nazi persecution of the Jews. He stopped short, however, of blaming the Church itself. He said that wrong or unfair interpretations of the New Testament had led to 'hostility' towards the Jews in the Christian world. Such prejudices, he said, had

> helped to deaden consciences, so that when the wave of persecutions inspired by a pagan anti-Semitism flooded Europe . . . the spiritual resistance of many was not what humanity had a right to expect on the part of the disciples of Christ . . . Anti-Semitism is without any justification and absolutely to be condemned. [*Jewish Chronicle,* 7 November 1997, p. 8]

The Pope's statement has stopped short of recognizing Christian responsibility for Jewish persecution. In this way it did not go as far as the recent statement by French bishops, which was more incisive and contrite. But it remains an important step and it is to be welcomed, especially in Poland where much of the theology seems to have remained unchanged, especially in rural areas. In November 1997, Father Henryk Jankowski, of the St Brygida Church in Gdansk, who was Solidarity's first chaplain, was suspended by his archbishop Tadeusz Goclowski for a year after saying that Jews have no place in his country's government. In a sermon he had said: 'the Jewish minority should not be accepted in our government', an apparent reference to the nomination of Bronislaw Geremek, who is of Jewish descent, as Foreign Minister in the new government. If Jews were to be 'tolerated' as a minority, they were not allowed to belong and they were to be denied any positions in the government of the country. These expressions of anti-Semitism are by no means unique to Poland and there were very familiar in pre-war Europe.

Sometimes assimilation into the dominant culture encouraged Jews to separate themselves from their Jewishness. In a recent lecture 'Was G.K. Chesterton anti-Semitic?' reported in the *Jewish Chronicle,* a powerfuln Labour shadow Foreign Secrretary, Gerald Kaufman, refused to accept that Chesterton's attitudes were somehow excusable because they were endemic to the times and symptomatic of the 'casual, unthinking anti-Semitism rife in popular conversation and literature'. He quoted a 1933 interview with the *Jewish Chronicle,* in which Chesterton condemned Hitler, but said that he still thought that there was a 'Jewish problem. What I understand by the expression of Jewish spirit is a spirit foreign in Western countries.' In an article elsewhere the same year, Chesterton had maintained that 'it was only just for Hitler to say that Jews had been too powerful in Germany' and that Jews 'had been involved in an obscure conspiracy against Christendom, which some of them can never abandon'. If Chesterton was a Zionist it was 'only because he refused to accept the possibility of Jews being patriots in other countries' (*Jewish Chronicle,* 14 November 1997, p. 8). As Kaufman concluded, 'his being a Zionist did not stop him from being anti-Semitic' (reported in the *Jewish Chronicle,* 14 November 1997, p. 8).

In the late 1940s Arthur Koestler had written an article saying that Jews had only two options: either to assimilate into gentile culture completely or to become Israelis in the new state of Israel. As Michael Ignatieff recognizes in an interview marking Isaiah Berlin's death:

> The Koestler article roused something important in Berlin. He thought Koestler's choice was entirely false: that there was an authentic way to be a Jew in a gentile society. For the rest of his life, he hated that antithesis, the idea that there are only two ways to go. [*Jewish Chronicle,* 14 November 1997, p. 30]

Ignatieff reports that Berlin always said that his Zionism came with his mother's milk. She was a passionate Zionist. Then, when he went to Palestine in the early 1930s he was moved to tears by the sight of Jewish officials in uniform. He had a passionate belief that the Jewish people couldn't be really at home unless they were within their own frontiers and had their own language.

The issue for Berlin was *cultural.* He had a fantastic sense that being at home, belonging somewhere, depends on living in a community where people understand not only what you say but what you *mean.*

He felt that Israel provided that for the Jewish people and he gave it a critical support all his life. But when his Israeli friends said, 'you must come to Israel, you belong here', he said 'I don't, I'm an Englishman.' He loved England and was devoted to it and he fought over these issues in his own mind all his life' (*Jewish Chronicle,* 14 November 1997, p. 30).

Notes

1. An account of the Nazi occupation of the Channel Islands and the implications this had for Jews who were living on the Islands has been

explored by Madeline Bunting Moyel, *Occupation: Channel Islands under German Rule, 1940–45* (London, Harper Collins, 1996).

2. The Nazi occupation of Poland was soon followed by plans to create a 'Jewish reservation' in an area near Lublin. Jews were moved there from different countries in Europe and forced to survive on their own. This plan proved to be impracticable given the large numbers of Polish Jews, so the policy was switched towards the creation of ghettos in the larger cities. It is significant that the Nazis themselves have written almost nothing about this 'reservation'. Only through neutral sources did it leak out that large numbers of Jews were being transferred from western Poland, Bohemia, and Austria to the Lublin area. As reported in *The German New Order in Poland* (London, Hutchinson & Co., 1943), quoting from the *Luxemburger Wort,* 21 November 1939:

> The haste with which the reservation has been established out of nothing is leading to desperate situations. Sometimes trains drive on for forty kilometres beyond Lublin and halt in the open country, where the Jews alight with their luggage and have to find themselves primitive accommodation in the surrounding villages. Up to November 10 about 45,000 Jewish men, women and children . . . have been sent to the reservation' [*The German New Order in Poland* (London, Hutchinson & Co., 1943), p. 232]

A letter written from Piaski, near Lublin, 8 March 1940, says

> It is still very cold here and a snowstorm is raging. We are quartered with co-religionists who, despite their poverty, are doing all they can to make us feel at home. But we would be very grateful if you could send us a little food and some old clothes, such as woollen socks, woollen shirts, etc. [*The German New Order in Poland* (London, Hutchinson & Co., 1943), p. 234]

3. One of the first accounts to draw upon interviews with the second generation was Helen Epstein's *Children of the Holocaust* (New York, G.P. Putnam, 1979). Different studies have followed in its wake.

4. For some helpful reflections upon the notion of a Jewish diaspora see Zygmunt Bauman, *Modernity and the Holocaust* (Cambridge, Polity', 1988). See also the discussion 'Negating the Diaspora: A Symposium', *Jewish Frontier* 47, No 10 (December 1979). For some interesting discussions about how notions of the diaspora have been extended to open up a discussion between Jews and Blacks, see Joseph E. Harris ed. *Global Dimensions of the African Diaspora* (Washington DC, Howard University Press, 1982) and Paul Gilroy, *The Black Atlantic* (London, Verso, 1993).

5. A useful introduction to the Talmud, which gives it an historical context, is Adin Steinsalz, *The Essential Talmud* (New York, J. Aronson, 1995).
6. Simone Weil explores the relationship of power and greatness within the West in *The Need for Roots* (London, Routledge, 1972).
7. Walter Benjamin questions a Hegelian notion of progress and the notions of history and time which it embodies in 'Theses on the Philosophy of History' in Hanna Arendt, *Illuminations* (London, Fontana Books, 1973). Benjamin was also invoking a Jewish messianic tradition in his writings, which he had learned about through his friendship with Gershom Scholem. See Gershom Scholem, *From Berlin to Jerusalem: Memories of my Youth*, trans. Harry Zohn (New York, Schoken Books, 1980) and also Gershom Scholem, *Walter Benjamin: The Story of A Friendship* (London, Faber & Faber, 1982).
8. The ways in which Jewish masculinities intersect with the dominant masculinities and the different ways in which men can be made to feel that their masculinities can never be taken for granted but have to be constantly proved is a theme I have explored in *Man Enough: Embodying Masculinities* (London, Sage, 1997).
9. A recent biography that attempts to explore Berlin's relationships to Jewishness, which was often not explicit in his teaching, is provided by Michael Ignatieff, *Isaiah Berlin* (London, Chatto & Windus, 1998). For a recent intellectual engagement with Berlin's ideas that attempts to place him in relation to a liberal tradition see John Gray, *Isaiah Berlin* (London, Harper Collins, 1995).
10. A sense of the breadth of Berlin's intellectual work and his sympathies for Herder and the Counter-Enlightenment can be found in Isaiah Berlin, *Against the Current* (Oxford, OUP, 1981).

5

Living with the Shadows

Complex Identities

We searched the records for evidence of the birth of Anna's father in Strzemieszyce in 1918. Anna felt a sense of anticipation as the official looked through the carefully handwritten records. But her hopes were to be dashed as he found no evidence and then told us what he already knew – that the Jewish records were kept separately. Apparently the registration of births and deaths was not in the hands of the impartial state but was a matter for religious authorities. He told us that when people died they were not buried in the town but in the Jewish cemetery in Bedzin.

It seemed as if there were few signs of the Jewish life that once thrived here before the war. This was a manifestation of the separation in which Jews lived. They were responsible for keeping all their records of birth and death. When so many of the synagogues were destroyed, records were also destroyed. If there had been gaps in shared records, at least people could be aware of those who had been lost.

The week before our visit, the Jewish-born Archbishop of Paris, Jean-Marie Lustiger, had just been made an honorary citizen of Bedzin, where his parents lived until 1917. His mother, the daughter of a Bedzin rabbi, perished in Auschwitz. Anna's father was born a year after they left Bedzin. Auschwitz is about a half-hour drive away in the car. It is difficult not to feel that people must have been aware of what was happening as their Jewish neighbours and friends were taken there. The area is now dominated by the heavy industry in Katowice and these surroundings towns have gradually been absorbed into its influence. It is an area that has witnessed a dramatic increase in population since the war. Archbishop Lustiger, who was born in Paris in 1926, converted to Catholicism at the age of 14. However he has never concealed his Jewish roots. Addressing a ceremony on Bedzin, he expressed the hope that 'This occasion should help to join together the once-severed thread of common culture and tradition between Catholics and Jews' (*Jewish Chronicle,* 14 November

1997, p. 6). During his trip he also visited a memorial to a local Catholic priest, Mieczyslaw Zawadski, who gave refuge to more than 100 Jews when the Nazis overran Bedzin. Anna's family was to find no such protection.

The Krakow ghetto had come into existence by 1941, although the Jews living outside town were not yet obliged to move into it.[1] Hania's father was a well-known figure in the streets of Olsza. He was a Talmud scholar who had never been able to provide for his family, however modestly. Her resourceful and hard-working mother took in washing and, until the war, she cooked for an elderly widower who was strictly kosher. Hania's father wanted to join his people in the ghetto for he believed that conditions both for prayer and study would be more congenial. As Janina Martinho recalls her childhood friendships in Krakow before the Nazi *Aktion* in which 6,000 Jews were rounded up and deported, 'He seemed absent minded and totally divorced from all things earthly. He was permanently conducting, so Hania told us, an inner, learned dialogue with his Maker' (*Jewish Chronicle,* 31 October 1997, p. 25). The Meir family moved into the ghetto in the early summer of 1941, when it was not so overcrowded. and they were allocated a room in an old lodging house in Wegierska Street. It was decent, quite spacious, and with a large window. 'Here, amid our own, we can breath freely', he said. 'We are safe, praise be to the Almighty' (*Jewish Chronicle,* 31 October 1997, p. 25).

But it was not to turn out that way. The Meir family survived the June 1942 *Aktion* intact. The ghetto was reduced to half its size as half of its original terrain was reclaimed. The Meir family was relocated to Lvovska Street. Janina remembers running into Hanis in the ghetto streets just once between the June and October 1942 *Aktions.* 'But it was not the same Hania. Life was being sapped out of her. She told me she belonged to the women's cleaning battalion, a labour contingent assigned to cleaning German Wehrmacht barracks. It was hard work. She was only just coping' (*Jewish Chronicle,* 31 October 1997, p. 25). 'And they shared their room in Lvovska Street with a godless, inconsiderate family who ate pork and left bones and scraps around knowing perfectly well that the Meiers were strictly kosher.'

Janina Martinho records what happened next, helping us to recognize the individuals who are suffering in these conditions. It is not a question of naming a 'mass deportation' but of the loss of individual lives that is so difficult to honour. This is not only a challenge to individual and collective memory, but to an Enlightenment tradition in its pervasive drive to subsume individual lives:

The Aktion of October 28, 1942 was sprung upon us without any warning. It resulted in thousands of the ghetto inhabitants being deported to their death.

Lvovska Street and the adjoining roads, which were the main target of the Aktion, became a ghost-town, their inhabitants, almost without exception, having been consigned to 'The East.'

In the following days, the ghetto grapevine accounted for every family, every individual lost. The tally was 6,000. A fearful cry ran along the crumbling, moss-covered walls – '6,000!' It rose from damp, mould infested cellars to cold, rain-dripping attics – '6,000!'

The Meirs? All four. The Sonnenscheins. Three generations of the Weinreb family: mother, daughter, two grandchildren. Old Mrs Zelinger and her middle-aged daughter, an *Arbeitsamt* clerk who chose to share her mother's fate – an unsung heroine. The painter Ralf Immergluck and his wife, Sara.

Twelve-year-old Irena Zuckermann, who hoped to find her mother; 19-year-old Joseph Fischler; 16-year-old Henryk Birnere; 20 year-old Barbara Reich. The Order couple with their three-year old son, Olek; 34-year-old Bronia Kunstlinger with her three children aged 11, nine and five . . . Six thousand human beings had been gathered in the Umschlagsplatz – the ghetto marshalling yard – and marched, under the SS guard's watchful eyes, to the cattle-trucks at Plaszow railway station.

Ada could only hobble, a few steps at a time. Was she tossed into a lorry, like a parcel, with the invalids, the infirm, the aged? Was she flung, like an inanimate object, into the cattle-truck with total strangers?

Or did her father, a giant of a man, carry his 12-year-old daughter in his arms all the way to Plaszow and enter the cattle-truck cuddling little Ada up to him?

I like to believe the latter. [Ada's Fate, *Jewish Chronicle,* 31 October 1997, p. 25]

Teaching our Children

Young children ask questions. Often they ask questions that we as adults are not prepared for. Often they want to know about their families and where they come from. Growing up in the second generation meant that our parents wanted us desperately to be 'normal' and they feared that we would be injured through this knowledge of the past.[2] Truth had not saved them and sometimes it was difficult for them to appreciate it as a value. They had to learn to tell the authorities what they wanted to hear if they were to have a chance to escape. Often they learned to tell their children what they wanted them to know. As children we often learned to keep our questions to ourselves, sometimes fearing to be called 'abnormal' by our parents. We learned to protect our parents, and unwittingly we learned to carry their pain for them.[3]

Often it was confusing. I know that I can still feel that I had a 'normal' childhood and I am still sometimes surprised at the reactions of others when I share some of my history. I desperately wanted it to be 'normal' for this is what our parents often expected of us. But often I did not feel the same as other children, even other Jewish children who had grown up in Anglo-Jewry. It was easy to internalize the blame and think it reflected something 'wrong' with me. So I learnt to conceal what I was feeling, for I did not want to give others ground to reject me. I learnt to be a good listener and I could often understand what was going on for friends emotionally, often better than they could grasp themselves. I became 'objective' in a way encouraged by the dominant culture and somehow I left my own experience behind. I lived in hiding, not really wanting in these years to know too much of what had happened to my family during the war. I thought that this was to do with history, not to do with the life I was creating for myself as a young man born in England.

It was only later, in my late twenties, that I slowly recognized that my life was shadowed by the experiences of my parents. I realized that I was being told what my parents wanted me to know, not what had really happened to them. The silences were difficult to bear, especially when we were told that it had nothing to do with us. We had no 'reason' to be upset or depressed, because we had supposedly had everything that a child could want. There was nothing exceptional about our histories and we were lucky enough to be well-provided for within the middle class. We were encouraged to look to the future and forget about the past. Often our families had done their best to forget and they did not want to be reminded by their children. This has begun to change as the survivors and refugees have less pressure to make a living and more time to themselves in their retirements. Memories begin to return and sometimes there is an urge to share with children before it is too late. But sometimes a conversation might be opened up with others, but still not with children. This can be hurtful. Anna's mother used to talk to me about her experience in labour camp and the way she was protected by associating with an orthodox group of young women. They could tell, for instance, whether new arrivals to the camp would have a chance to survive by the way they ate their first meal. But she never shared these memories with Anna.

When Anna's mother visited us in London a few years before she died I went with her to a talk by Primo Levi who was talking about his own experience in the camps. This was one of the very few visits that Primo Levi made to London and he was talking at Yakar, an educational centre in north London about his experiences in the camps. He wanted to affirm that there good deeds that were also performed by some people able to maintain a sense of their human dignity in the most extreme conditions. Anna's mother found this hard to accept for she felt that moral values had been turned upside down as the camp represented a kind of hell. People stole from each other and nobody could trust anyone. If this went against her own experience in her group of young orthodox women, it was somehow important to believe this generalized vision of her experience. As other times she had recognized that some of the women guards had also shown kindness to them and respected their religious feelings but this had no place in the general picture that she had. It was a difficult evening but also one I was glad to have shared with her. But when we got home and Anna asked about it, her mother was very dismissive. 'What do you want to know? You aren't interested.' This was hurtful but she could not reach out to her daughter and share her experience. She could only reject.

I remember, as Daniel was growing up, trying to think about an appropriate time to share some of this history with him. We would put it off, rarely feeling that the time was right to share histories of the Shoah, not wanting his life to be somehow overshadowed in the ways ours had been. Anna and I had different responses. Anna, coming from a survivor family, felt that the time was later, when he might ask questions himself. I could feel that if he asked, at whatever age, he should be answered. (During this period I learnt a great deal from attending a seminar at the Steinberg Centre in north London with a survivor concerned about talking to young children about the Holocaust.) I knew how hard I had to struggle for any truth in my own family, so it was a value with which I deeply identified. But of course we both had to work on our own histories, and our feelings about Jewishness and the war. It was only if we could work emotionally on these issues for ourselves that we might be able to talk more openly when the time came. Again we had to take responsibility for our own emotional work, rather than focus upon a question of age. Anna found some wonderful stories, particularly about the rescue of Danish Jews and these helped to begin a conversation.

Of course children are different, and as parents you learn to recognise their individualities. Daniel and Lily had their own questions and they needed to be responded too appropriately. But it was not a matter of a 'right time' but of recognizing different ways that histories can be shared and questions honestly answered. It was a matter of opening up communication between Anna and myself on these issues, and this was often difficult. We had to respect our own timing and the different ways we might want to work on our histories. Often it is a slow process of unfolding that cannot be pressured. We had to learn to respect each other's sensitivities and different ways of working on ourselves. I know that I can sometimes pressure when I am unsure about something myself. Often there are unresolved issues that are emerging but, rather than deal with them, it can be tempting to project it onto others. Our different histories meet but they can also clash. Anna can feel that her experience as a child of survivors has absolutely no connection with what my family might have gone through. But these feelings have drifted away as we have discovered different ways of working on our issues and also supporting each other.

At some level it is striking that we fell in love with each other in the 1970s. I had grown up in England and she was on a visit from Brazil, not expecting to stay. It was a meeting that was to radically transform both our lives as we decided that we wanted to be with each other. There were profound cultural differences between Brazil and England to do with intimacy and relationship that we had to learn to negotiate. We were both Jewish, but we had very different diasporic experiences of Jewishness as I was to discover when I visited Brazil in 1976 to find a different kind of Jewish community that included large numbers of camp survivors.

There were some survivors in England but, as I have said, they tended to be more scattered and, for many years in England, they learned not to talk about their experience as Kitty Hart makes clear in *Return to Auschwitz* (London, Sidgwick & Jackson, 1981). She recalls the advice given by her uncle when she came as a child to England. They told her not to talk to anyone about her experience because they did not really want to know and would only feel embarrassed. She learned to keep her history to herself, not sharing it with her own family until they had grown up. Kitty Hart gave a number of talks in London in the mid 1980s partly based on her experience in Auschwitz and the film she was to make for Yorkshire TV about a trip she made with her son to the camp. She makes clear how difficult it was in the early post-war years to share her experiences in the camps. It seemed as if a veil of silence had fallen over the past, as people seemed to only want to look to the future. In England people wanted to put the war behind them and it was not till the 1980s that things began to change. All of a sudden she found that people wanted to listen and this helped her to value her own experience at last. It helped her open up a conversation with her own children.

Jewish Diasporas

As we reconnect to the lives that Jews lived in pre-war Poland and Lithuania, as well as in other countries in central and Eastern Europe, we can individually begin to feel that we have a past that does not stop but somehow predates and goes through the Shoah. This has not been easy for me to experience because I felt, until very recently, that there was a gap that could not be bridged. There was no bridge to the past. This made a difference to how I could root myself in the present. I did not really think about having Jewish-Polish ancestors, or how much of what I had learnt of as 'Jewish' was also shared as 'Polish'. But there are very different Jewish-Polish diasporas. There is the Zionist diaspora that comes to refocus itself in Israel, and there is also the tradition of the socialist Bund that was closely identified with a secular Poland and a Yiddish culture.[4] There were also religious Zionist traditions and assimilationist traditions that would have chosen to grow in Poland where they had been for a millennium.

As Britain learns to recognize itself as a multicultural society there is more space given to different 'races' and ethnicities. There is not the same pressure to assimilate into a dominant white Christian culture. There is no longer a single way of being 'English' or 'British' to which people feel they have to adapt. There is a growing recognition of different diasporas, as people learn to value living across different boundaries.[5] It is no longer a matter of having to decide where your loyalties rest for there is more space in which to validate difference and acknowledge that you can have different loyalties to different places and traditions. The attempt by Norman Tebbitt to critique a multicultural Britain and to set in place a homogenized notion of 'British' history was firmly rejected by Hague and the Tory leadership as the views of a 'dinosaur' at the 1997 Conservative Party conference in Blackpool. This reflects a shift in political culture that was very evident in the aftermath of Princess Diana's death.

Rather than feeling shamed by complex identities, young people have learned to value a double consciousness and create hybrid identities. Young people have been engaged in attempts to balance the values of traditional cultures with the freedoms offered by modernity. This is not an easy task and sometimes painful choices have to be made. As new black British identities are being forged, so British Asian identities are being struggled with as young women and men also redefine their gender and sexual relations with each other. Young British Jews are also taking a space to find a new relationship with their histories, but also with their diverse Jewish identities in Britain. There is a move towards recognition of diversity within religious and spiritual traditions that is still being resisted. There have been attempts to present feminism and gay liberation as if they were movements that were external to Jewish tradition, rather than recognize how they share, especially in their validation of the body and emotional life, particular traits with Jewish challenges to an Enlightenment vision of modernity. [6]

As Michael Ignatieff recalls when speaking of Isaiah Berlin's concern with identity, ethics and modernity:

> They are tragic choices because there isn't a science of politics; you have to make these choices with as full a sense of the reality of a situation as you can . . . He insisted that moral choice depends on something intuitive, what he called 'a sense of reality.' There's a realism and a moral depth to his politics which will survive. [*Jewish Chronicle,* 14 November 1997, p. 30]

But if Berlin stops short of considering the ways in which Jewish traditions can provide a challenge to modernity in the different ways that Rosenzweig and Levinas suggest, he does put his trust in people being free to make choices for themselves.[7] In this way he challenges the authority of any religious tradition that would seek to legislate what is good for others. He did not believe in a divine plan that has been laid out in advance and to which people have to conform. If there are commandments, these are to aid people in establishing a deeper connection with themselves and to give guidance to moral decisions that people can make for themselves. People will also suffer if they act immorally because at some level they will lose a connection with themselves.

Many Jews growing up in the post-war world have chosen to turn their backs on Judaism, which they see as having somehow 'failed' because of the destruction of European Jewry. They see its values as having been disproved so that there has to be a new beginning. In some ways this thinking is tacitly encouraged by Zionism and the replacement of Yiddish with Hebrew. But this is a false choice that did not need to be made as people in Israel and the diaspora have increasingly acknowledged in their attempt to redefine their relationship. It serves to uproot Jews from their histories and cultures – histories and cultures that could otherwise enrich their lives and experience. We still live in the shadows of Auschwitz. It has taken more than forty years in a frozen wilderness of denial to begin to come to terms with what happened in the war and to appreciate its centrality to the self-understanding of Western culture. The scars have barely healed and the surviving generation will soon all be dead. We need to learn from them before it is too late, but we also need to open up a dialogue between Judaism and the Christian world of modernity. For the Holocaust was not just a tragedy for the Jews. As a Liberal rabbi, Dr Sidney Brichto, put it recently in a letter to the Jewish Chronicle

The Holocaust was a crime against humanity and human civilisation of which the Jews – because of the history of anti-Semitism – were the prime victims.

Our attempt should not be to parochialise Yom Hashoah, but to invite the entire civilised world to join us in its observance. We need it as a constant reminder of what happens when one group decides to ignore the fact that those they destroy have a human face just as they do. [*Jewish Chronicle,* 14 November 1997, letters, p. 28]

Before we can offer an invitation, however, we have to find ways of relating to what happened ourselves. As adults we have to do this difficult emotional and cultural work if we are to be able to share more openly and honestly with our children. This is one of the reason that Jews from all over the world are visiting Poland. But it should not be simply to visit Jewish sites of destruction, but also to value the traditions and cultures that once survived there. Rather than splitting from the Yiddish cultures of the past, we have to honour them and share their gifts with our children. This is part of an inheritance that we should not allow to be shamed. This would give a victory to Fascism, which so often sought to demean Jewish traditions and culture in the eyes of Jews. We need to value forms of spiritual resistance, which have too often been discounted as forms of resistance to power.

The words of the head of the Slabodka Musar-Yeshiva, Rabbi Nachum Yanchiker still echo. This was the last Musar (ethical) talk he gave, moments before the German invasion:

With the full weight of the authority granted to me as your Rabbi, I command you to leave me here. You must flee and save yourselves ! Take heed of your bodies and your souls. Do not place your lives in danger unnecessarily because of the lightning bolt that strikes from without, but do not think for one fleeing instant that you must sacrifice your lives for your inner spiritual matters. I beseech and adjure you to remember always those of our people who feel at the hands of the murderers. It is not for man to judge which one of them shall be a saint and which note. Everyone slaughtered by the wicked ones is to be judged a saint. My dear students, always remember the Neared of Lithuania, the Yeshiva of Slabodka. And when the world returns again to stability and quiet, never become weary of teaching the glories, the wisdom, the Torah and the Musar of Lithuania, the beautiful and ethical life which Jews lived here. Do not become embittered by wailing and tears. Speak of these matters with calmness and serenity, as did our holy Sages in the Midrash, 'Lamentations Rabbati'. And so as your hold Sages have done – pour forth your words and cast them into letters. This will be the greatest retribution which you can wreak upon these wicked ones. Despite the raging wrath of our foes the holy souls of your brothers and sisters will then remain alive. These evil ones schemed to blot out their names from the face of the earth; but a man cannot destroy letters. For words have wings; they mount up to the heavenly heights and endure for eternity. [*Forms of Prayer: Days of Awe,* Reform Synagogues of Great Britain, London, 1985]

For many families who survived the war these traditions were not to be remembered, but rather to be consciously forsaken. Even where parents spoke Yiddish between themselves, they often chose not to pass this on to their children. They wanted their children to 'become English' for this was the path to safety and assimilation. This was very much the aspiration in the 1950s. Mothers might speak Yiddish to their partners, but discourage their sons and daughters because it only made life difficult with the fear of anti-Semitism.

One man shared his experience growing up in post-war Liverpool, at a recent gathering in London to mark the centenary of the Bund. He refused to blame his parents because he acknowledged the pressure they were under but he did regret that the Jewish schools had taken a clear political decision that Yiddish would not be taught alongside modern Hebrew. Their identification with Zionism was, sadly, deemed to be threatened by an honouring of Yiddish tradition and culture. The lines were drawn. It was only the Chasidic community that was to retain Yiddish as a living language and this was partly because Hebrew was deemed to be the spiritual language that was not for everyday usage. The Bund had also remained loyal to Yiddish as the language of the diaspora. They were socialists who believed in ethnic minorities being able to sustain their own language and culture. They fought for the right of Jews to live in the Diaspora and they played a crucial part in the resistance to Nazism.[8]

The Bund was a secular movement and it identified with *Yiddishkeit* as a cultural tradition, but it also thought that Jewish particularity was temporary as the movement's internationalism was centred around the possibilities of 'uniting the human race'. Sometimes this meant that they could underestimate the depth of peoples' involvement in cultural traditions as sources of identity and belonging. At times it shared the universalist vision that differences would wither away as a common humanity would be reasserted. It shared Enlightenment beliefs in the identification of history with progress, but at some level it failed to appreciate the different ways of thinking the relationship between 'particularism' and 'universality' that were embodied within the prophetic traditions of Judaism and that implicitly served as a challenge to an Enlightenment vision of modernity. The Bund was sometimes militant in its secularism and it saw Jewish religious traditions as forms of superstition that would give way with the progress of scientific rationalism. In this way they were very much a movement of their time. The remnants that survived the Shoah need to think in different terms if they are to remain a vital force able to inspire a younger generation. In part it means coming to terms with the re-visioning of socialism and the complexities of Israeli society in its relationship with diverse diaspora communities.

Books and Traditions

Sheila Shulman, a rabbi in the reform movement, was asked at the same London gathering marking the centenary of the Bund, to participate in a discussion on whether there could be a future for a secular Jewish tradition. She rightly refused the simplistic terms in which the debate was framed. She wanted to explore ideas and she shared how she had come from a Bundist background herself and definitely had more in common with the egalitarian aspirations of the Bund than she did with most orthodox Jews. But she made the point that the distinction between the 'secular' and the 'sacred' was itself a Christian distinction that made little sense within the Jewish tradition. Judaism refused to recognize a distinction between the 'spiritual' and the 'material', for everyday life was infused with the spiritual. The earthly was not regarded as the profane that needed to be transcended if we are to aspire to the 'spiritual'. Rather the task is to make everyday life holy through struggling to bring greater justice and righteousness into the world. We were not, as within Christian tradition, to treat the body and sexuality as part of an 'animal' nature that we needed, in Kant's terms to 'rise above' and so as no part of our humanity.

Judaism spoke for a different kind of humanism and, as Rosenzweig recognized in his call for a new thinking. As I have learned to think about it, the body and sexuality do not reflect the 'sins of the flesh' as they do within Christianity. This was always part of the accusation made by the established Church against 'carnal Israel'.[9] Rather Judaism served as a fundamental challenge to an Enlightenment vision of modernity, which was cast within the terms of secularized Protestant tradition through its insistence that our bodies and sexualities are 'part of' who we are as human being and so exist as expressions of our humanity. As I have already argued, this echoes some of the feminist challenges to modernity, which also refuse notions of personal identity identified with the disembodied rational self of a Cartesian tradition, and so opens up the possibilities of a more creative dialogue between Judaism and feminism. In different ways traditional Judaism has developed as a patriarchal tradition and has often served to silence women and limit their education and spiritual expression, but we have to be careful not to blame Judaism for somehow bringing patriarchal assumptions into an otherwise more egalitarian Christian tradition.[10] This is a dangerous misreading of the sources that can unwittingly sustain new forms of Christian anti-Semitism.

A central insight of Biblical Judaism is that men and women are made in the image of G-d. In our sexualities and genders we are also made in the image of G-d – even if this is often traditionally interpreted in patriarchal and heterosexist terms – and if we have to sometimes struggle with sexual desires in diverse forms this does not make them 'animal' and unholy. Rather, within the Jewish tradition they are crucially an expression of love. This is quite different from the Christian 'pure' love as a love that is untainted by sexuality. Within modernity the position of love was taken by reason, and 'pure' reason was to become a reason that was untainted by emotions and desires. Rather than learning from embodied emotions and desires as we do in the all-too-human stories in the Hebrew Bible of, for instance, Abraham and Sarah, Cain and Abel, Isaac and Jacob in their struggles to experience G-d, we often learn to devalue the difficult choices they are forced to make. We learn within a dominant Christian tradition that there is a single path to be followed, not a diversity of paths we have to choose between. As Berlin recognizes, it was a strength of the Romantic tradition in the West to remind us that there is not always a single answer to any question that can be discerned through reason alone, as the Enlightenment view has it.[11] People might make different choices for themselves and there might be equally valid responses to the same question.

But as Jews growing up within a dominant Christian society we have often learned to construe our Jewishness through Christian eyes. This has affected the relationship we have been able to develop with traditional Jewish texts. Rather than welcome the Tenach and the Talmud as part of a shared inheritance of the book, as providing stories and narratives through which Jewish people have sought to make sense of their experience for generations, we have been encourage to think that if we do not 'believe in the divine' then we cannot approach these narratives. But there is no sharp distinction that Judaism makes between narratives that are 'sacred' and narratives that are 'profane'. Interpretations are not given, but they are always worked for and it is crucial in the tradition that they are read against the issues that emerge in peoples' lives. These books are part of Jewish history and tradition but no sharp line is drawn with other narratives, such as the Yiddish stories of Mendel, Peretz, Shalom Aleichem or Singer, that we can equally illuminate the lives we live. Of course orthodox traditions give a particular authority to the Tenach which is taken to be the 'word of G-d', but even here it has always been an open issue – more open than Jewish fundamentalist pretend – of *how* these texts are to be interpreted. The meanings these texts offer are the illuminations that they can bring to our lives, possibly bringing us into a deeper connection with ourselves in relation to spirituality.

Only in engaging with these texts can we learn from them for the lives we live. What we discover is different views expressed and a refusal to foreclose judgement. Texts to not come with a given interpretation that has to be accepted as a matter of faith. For Judaism religion has never been a matter of a belief in G-d, which then explains participation in religious practices. Deeds come first, as the lines in Exodus express it, and understanding follows – 'in the beginning was the deed'. This was a crucial insight for the later philosophical work of Wittgenstein and explains why he saw his later philosophical work as 'Hebraic' as opposed to Greek. There were no ideal patterns given to which human beings have to learn to conform. The Greeks presented certain ideals which human beings had to aspire to, or else feel bad about themselves. They felt unworthy and in Christian terms, sinful. They constantly had to aspire to live spiritual lives because this was an expression of a 'higher' sense of self. But they could only do this if they struggled against their base 'animal' natures. But within the Hebrew tradition there were no ideals against which everyday life was to be compared and found wanting. Rather it was through following the details of everyday experience, that difficult moral choices were to be made. We could look to the Biblical narratives for examples, but we have to make decision for ourselves. Possibly Berlin was unwittingly echoing a Jewish tradition in his recognition that these choices could not be made through reason alone. Individuals had the freedom to make choices for themselves.

One response to Sheila Shulman was given by a woman who was in an inter-faith marriage. She had felt a need to explore Jewish history and culture. This had led her to want to know something about the religious traditions and sometimes she felt a need to attend services. Her husband, brought up in a Christian tradition, could not understand this at all. He thought it was quite irrational if she did not 'believe in G-d' to want to attend services. He thought this was hypocritical because the prayers could not possibly have any meaning for her unless she already had some kind of faith. As far as he was concerned belief was prior and was always a matter of faith and conviction. But this has never been the Jewish path and she found it difficult to explain the impulses that were moving her. The tradition recognizes, through a process of *teshuva* – religious practice – that we might only make a spiritual connection for a short moment, before we again feel quite distant and removed. This process of spiritual struggle was something with which Jacob was also struggling, and it is part of the meaning the story of Jacob and the ladder can offer us.

Many people who have grown up in orthodox traditions can be left feeling that the tradition has to be oppressive and does not allow people to really think for themselves. They had not been offered freedom and thoughtfulness, even if the religious sources could offer this. This is especially true for women who have long felt silenced by the orthodox traditions, unable to have the recognition and status that their brothers enjoyed. Women are no longer prepared to be 'second class citizens' when it comes to religion, now that they enjoy greater equality within secular society. They can feel that the religion has very little to offer them and if they want to pass on Jewish traditions to their children, they have to do it in secular ways that offer more equality in relation to gender and sexuality. Issues of homosexuality have only slowly between confronted in the progressive movements and orthodoxy generally remains unmoved in relation to sexual politics. The hopes that accompanied Jonathan Sachs's talk of a decade of Jewish renewal in Britain have been largely dashed because he has been unable to accept the pluralism for which he otherwise argues.

The divisions that separate religious Jews only serve to distance those who identity was secular. The terrible unease that followed the assassination of Rabin and the divisions that it showed in Israeli society have hardly healed but it seems, with the revival of the peace process, as if people have learned something from the experience and have come together in tolerance. Orthodoxy seemed to be taking some responsibility for helping to create a climate in which hate could thrive. But the moves towards Jewish fundamentalism, often deriving from within the secular cultures of the United States, do not seem to have learned the lessons. The pluralism that existed in the pre-war communities could serve as an example of tolerance and respect. At some level it is difficult not to feel that the fragmentations within the Jewish world also have something to do with the difficulties of coming to terms with the Shoah. The wilful determination that it will not happen again has too often been tied to a disdain for the traditions that went before. There were differences between orthodox movements, especially with the challenges provided by Chasidism, but there was also a certain tolerance. At that time the tradition seemed to work to help in sustaining some respect for differences.

Rather than presenting a vision of homogenized community to the outside world, which has often served as a form of self-regulation on the part of Jewish elites who have seen it as their responsibility to speak for the community, we should recognize the diversity of Jewish voices. This should be treated as a sign of strength rather than weakness. There were always different schools, as Hillel and Shamai represented different approaches to Biblical interpretation. If a choice had to be made between them, for Hillel it did not invalidate the arguments that were made for different positions. If we are to create more inclusive traditions, we have somehow to come to terms with the Shoah and the spiritual and political traditions that were lost. Rather than treating them as a sign of weakness and a mark of shame, we have to learn to revalue them so that they are honoured as part of a shared inheritance. This involves opening up a conversation between different generations, but also between different communities as new forms of Jewish expression begin to find voice in Poland, Russia, Hungary and other countries in central and eastern Europe. If not now, when?

Notes

1. In the Polish Ministry of Information publication *The German New Order in Poland* (London, Hutchinson, 1943), there is a description of the establishment of the ghetto in Krakow. Originally the Germans had 'intended to expel the Jews from Cracow altogether, and in fact a large number were so expelled. Later a decision was taken to leave 20,000 Jews in the city. Part of a suburb of Cracow, Podgorze, situated on the right bank of the river Vistula, has been assigned as the ghetto area. The Poles living in this area has been ordered to shift to other parts of the city' (p. 241). But a decree published in the *Krakauer Zeitung* of 6 March 1941 established a special closed ghetto district in Krakow. As the decree has it: 'In the urban district of Cracow a closed Jewish area is to be established with immediate effect. All Jews living in this town are compelled to move to this area. No Jew will be allowed to live outside the Jewish area' (quoted in Polish Ministry of Information, *The German New Order in Poland* (London, Hutchinson, 1943 p. 242)).

2. The ways in which children were to be protected from learning about the Shoah is a theme explored in *The Memorial Candles: Children of the Holocaust* (London, Routledge, 1992).

3. The ways in which children learn to take responsibility for their parents is a theme explored for the second generation in *The Aftermath: Living*

with the Holocaust (Cambridge, Cambridge University Press, 1995) and Dan Bar-On *Fear's Hope: Three Generations of the Holocaust* (Cambridge, Harvard University Press, 1995).

4. For an illuminating exploration of the diverse social and political movements which existed in pre-war Poland see Nora Levin's *While Messiah Tarries: Jewish Socialist Movements 1870–1917* (New York, Schocken Books, 1977).

5. For discussions about the changing character of nationhood and citizenship within a multicultural society, see, for instance, Marshall Berman, *All that is Solid Melts into Air* (London, Verso, 1983); Paul Gilroy, *There Aint No Black in the Union Jack: The Cultural Politics of Race and Nation* (London, Hutchinson, 1987); Catherine Hall, *White, Male and Middle Class* (Cambridge, Polity, 1992), and Werner Sollors, *Beyond Ethnicity* (New York and Oxford, OUP,1986).

6. While insightful in many ways about the Enlightenment tradition, Jonathan Sachs, chief rabbi with a background in teaching philosophy, has strongly resisted an engagement with feminism and gay liberation. Whilst valuing pluralism he resists it when it comes to a Jewish tradition. See, for instance, Jonathan Sachs, *The Persistence of Faith: Religion, Morality and Society in a Secular Age* (London, Weidenfeld & Nicolson, 1991).

7. A very insightful study that draws out interesting connections and contrasts between Rosenzweig and Levinas is Richard A. Cohen, *Elevations: The Height of the Good in Rosenzweig and Levinas* (Chicago, University of Chicago Press, 1994). For a study that helps to place their writings in a historical and cultural context see Susan A. Handelman, *Fragments of Redemption: Jewish Thought and Literary Theory in Benjamin, Scholem and Levinas* (Bloomington, Indiana University Press, 1991). For a more specific exploration of themes in Rosenzweig's work see Paul Mendes-Flohr (ed.), *The Philosophy of Franz Rosenzweig* (Hanover, University Press of New England, 1988).

8. For a brief history of the Bund and the ways it developed see Nora Levin, *While Messiah Tarries: Jewish Socialist Movements 1890–1917,* New York, Schocken Books, 1977.

9. The ways in which traditional Judaism has thought about the body and sexuality and the contrast with dominant Christian traditions are explored in Daniel Boyarin, *Carnal Israel: Reading Sex in Talmudic Judaism* (Berkeley, University of California Press, 1993). The different ways in which Judaism has conceived of sexuality are explored in their historical context by David Biale, *Eros and the Jews* (New York,

Basic Books, 1992) and Howard Eilberg-Schwartz (ed.) *People of the Body: Jews and Judaism from an Embodied Perspective* (Albany, New York University Press, 1992).

10. The ways in which some feminist theology has too readily identified Judaism as the source of patriarchal masculinity within a dominant Christian tradition is explored in Judith Plaskow *Standing Again at Sinai: Judaism from a Feminist Perspective* (San Franciso, Harper Collins, 1990).

11. Isaiah Bellin explores tensions between an enlightenment and romantic traditions in essays collected in *Against the Current* (Oxford, Oxford University Press, 1981).

– 6 –

Out of the Ruins of Memory

'And Jacob sent messengers before him to Esau his brother.' Genesis 32:4

Angels

Louis Jacobs reminds us that in the Bible the word *malach* sometimes means a human messenger – anyone sent to carry out an act on behalf of someone else. Hence the translation in the King James version of *malachim* as the plural form in our verse. But it also means an angel, a messenger of God, the explicit meaning in a previous verse, where Jacob meets *malachei elohim*. As Jacobs explains

> The Midrash, consequently has two opinions on those sent by Jacob. According to one opinion he sent human messengers, presumably because he would not have sent the angels he had encountered to do his bidding.
>
> According to the other opinion, quoted by Rashi, Jacob sent actual malachim – malachim mamash, an interesting expression, denoting that, by the time of the Midrash, the word malach had come to mean 'angel' in its usual connotation. [*Jewish Chronicle,* 12 December 1997, p. 23]

Medieval Jewish works often discuss how 'actual' are 'actual angels' – what reality are we referring to when we speak of angels? For Maimonides, angels are purely spiritual forces used by God for the fulfilment of God's purposes.[1] This means that the biblical references to angels in human form are references to appearances in a dream. Spiritual forces are disembodied and can be seen as human beings only in the imagination produced by a dream. For Maimonides, Jacob did not really wrestle with the angel but only dreamed that he did. But for the Zohar, a primary source for Kaballah, angels can actually appear as human beings, although only when they have assumed corporal form. Otherwise, as Louis Jacobs explains it, 'they could not be contained within the physical universe' (*Jewish Chronicle,* 12 December 1997, p. 23).

Whatever 'reality' we give to angels, there is a sense that, for post-Holocaust Jews, we are almost inevitably touched by history. We might escape it for a while, and we might choose to think that history exists in the past and therefore has little relevance or meaning for the lives we live in the present. This tendency to split from the past is often reinforced within post-modern cultures. As African-Americans often do not want to be reminded of the heritage of slavery, so often American Jews do not really want to have to relate to the Shoah. Often the 'past' is imagined as a burden that compromises the freedom that people can realize in the present. Within an Enlightenment vision of modernity we learn, in Kant's terms, that the past is a form of unfreedom and determination that we have to separate from if we are to live as free and autonomous human beings in the present.[2]

We are encouraged, in the name of freedom, to forsake the past. We are reassured that the past can be left to others, as we focus upon living as best we can in the present. We do not want to recognize the angels that we carry, nor do we often want to listen to the voices of the past. We do not want to struggle with Benjamin's angels of history, searching through the remains of the past to discover meanings for the present.[3]

As Susan Handelman reminds us in *Fragments of Redemption: Jewish Thought and Literary Theory* (Bloomington, Indiana University Press, 1991, p. 168) Benjamin constantly invokes the presence of angels: 'In the 1931 essay on Kraus, Benjamin also refers to Klee's New Angel, "who preferred to free men by taking from them, rather than make them happy by giving to them," as an image for Karl Kraus's mission of purifying language and society through destructive critique.' Benjamin's Kraus essay concludes with the image of the new angel:

> Perhaps one of those who, according to the Talmud, are at each moment created anew in countless throngs, and who, once they have raised their voices before God, cease and pass into nothingness. Lamenting, chastising, rejoicing? No matter – in this evanescent voice the ephemeral work of Kraus is modelled. Angelus – that is the messenger of the old engravings. [Peter Demetz (ed.), *Reflections,* (New York, Harcourt Brace, 1978), p. 273]

Within the modern West we often grow up with a belief in progress. This means that whatever was of value in the past is somehow preserved within the present. This allows us to take refuge in the present and deafens us to the voices of the past. We do not want to hear their pain, for we learn to accept that the suffering was somehow justified in the progress that it prepared for the present. These sacrifices in the name of visions of historical progress were often integral to nineteenth-century notions of science and progress.[4] Within both liberalism and orthodox Marxism we learned that history could somehow be identified with progress. If we learned to identify sufferings in the past, we could explain them as sacrifices that helped to bring a 'better' present into being. But this belief in progress, shared by the emancipated Jewish communities in Western Europe, made it difficult for them to believe the terrible fate that was being prepared for them, even when they could witness it gathering around them. At some level they felt that they would be protected by their own angels, for they had come to believe in the progress offered by modernity. In Western Europe they had come to believe, despite the traditions of anti-Semitism, that they were not a people set apart. This might have been felt in Poland and the Pale, but in Germany, where the Jews were proud of the medals they had gained in the First World War, they felt they were German citizens who happened to have Mosaic religious beliefs. As I hjave argued, this was the promise of a liberal vision of modernity.

Many Jews in Western Europe had grown up within traditions of scientific rationalism. They could no longer believe in angels and they were careful to read the Jewish texts, according to Mendelssohn. They were anxious to prove the rationality of their beliefs and the universalism of their aspirations.[5] They were ready to secularize or universalize the Jewish prophetic tradition almost to the point of dejudaization. The price seemed worth paying because Jews in Western Europe were feeling that they had at last established roots that they could believe in. The middle classes were feeling that they were free and equal citizens within the nation state. Citizenship was to provide the core of their identities and they were to learn to treat their Jewishness as incidental, as if were a matter of individual belief alone. They happened to have particular religious beliefs but this would not be allowed to stand in the way of the freedom and equality that they knew as citizens.[6] This created its own position of superiority that enabled these 'Enlightened' Jews to look down and in many ways despise their Eastern European 'co-religionists', who might still believe in angels. They had left these superstitions behind as they had become 'modern'. They were closely identified with traditions of scientific rationalism and they learned to separate themselves from and disdain 'Eastern' Jews. They felt that they were 'backward' and 'uncivilized' and they did not welcome their immigration into Western Europe, which they felt would threaten the position they had established. They learned to blame them for whatever anti-Semitism still existed in Austria and Germany, feeling that if they did not insist upon dressing differently, or drawing attention to their own traditions and rituals, then they would not give 'reasons' for people to be anti-Semitic. At some level this meant that Jews were divided against themselves, between 'West' and 'East'. They learned to blame each other for the emergence of anti-Semitism, Polish Jews thinking that if Jews had not pretended to be other than what they are they might have been left alone.

Shadows

Community has been made difficult for Jews since the Shoah. It can be difficult to for them to feel that they belong, for at some level they can still feel prepared for the knock on the door. Perhaps this is more readily felt by those who have been displaced. I was born in England but I am less sure than when I was a child whether this makes me 'English'. In some ways I feel terribly English, having been educated in England for most of my life, and when I go abroad this can remind me of ways I am English I might otherwise overlook. It might be different for young Jews who have been here for generations, who can feel a different sense of belonging. As England learns to come to terms with a multicultural reality, more space is created for diverse identities and there is more tolerance for different ways that people can feel 'at home'. John Silkin who was possibly the most significant Anglo-Jewish poet since Isaac Rosenberg, lived and died a proud, militant Jew. Silkin wrote of the late A.C. Jacobs (*Jewish Chronicle*, 12 December 1997, p. 22): 'Having a minority consciousness, he could sit himself nowhere . . . There was no home except in his speech and written language.' But there was, 'in the end, a place in the poem itself . . . one existing in a sense of community.' As Anthony Rudolf comments in his obituary: 'This difficult acceptance of community was a Jewish acceptance of Jewish community for Jacobs, and for Silkin, too' (*Jewish Chronicle,* December 12, 1997, p. 22).

Sometimes we can blame ourselves for feeling different from others, thinking that it reflects something 'wrong with us'. Growing up in the shadows of the Shoah, it can be difficult to register how awkward and uneasy this can still make us feel as Jews. There is a question mark over our own survival and the survival of our families, for often these questions are unconsciously passed on. The questions that one generation refuses to voice, are often passed on silently and taken into the bodies of the next generation. But there is also a terrible anger at what happened and at the sufferings of one's family. I have learned to express some of this, but so much still seems to remain as part of an endless stream. This anger can feel strangely at odds with the aspiration, which was so strong in the 1950s, to 'be normal'. This can still bother me as I watch some of the responses as I tell some of my family stories, for it can be difficult for me to register how 'different' some of these stories are. For me it was part of 'normal' family life, although at some level I had registered that my family history was far from normal, since for one thing it was not 'normal' to grow up knowing that uncles, aunts and cousins had been killed by the Nazis. But we learned to live with this knowledge 'as if' it were 'normal'.

In different ways we learned to discount and cover over what we knew as children, because we came to know many things that children were not supposed to know, listening to the adult conversations that we were not supposed to understand. We lived with death and with murder, even if at the same time we remained numb to their realities. We learned to know, but at some level not to feel or to talk about. We learned not to ask questions, which we knew would only cause further distress to our parents. We wanted to be 'normal' for them, as if this were a gift that we could give to them and that might help assuage their pain. We also knew that they were doing their best to be 'normal' for us. They wanted us to be 'happy' and they were willingly carrying their burdens so that we supposedly could have an easier life, which might redeem their lives in turn. But often they did not realize how much they passed on to the second generation, through not really sharing their experiences. We took it into our bodies, as if it were food.

Sometimes there was a dim awareness that they could not really love in ways that other mothers and fathers could love. This was the emotional damage following the historical trauma of terror and displacement that had been done and it could not be repaired easily. At some level knowing this they resolved to give their love in other ways, through food and presents. This is why it became so important to eat, to ingest, and take in the food they offered. We learned to eat without question, and if we were not hungry we learned to eat all the same because to refuse food was taken as a rejection of love and it was too much to bear, for love could not be given more directly. Food became charged and often the atmosphere around the dinner table was tense and uneasy. It was usually around meals that the bitterest arguments broke out, my mother blaming Leo, our stepfather for somehow wanting to rob the food from our mouths if he allowed us to leave food uneaten. Very quickly the tensions intensified and my mother lost control, as if at some level it was a life-and-death struggle for her. If we would not eat, we could not survive and she would have failed us. She would not let anything stand in the way.

In the years after the war we were surrounded by shadows. As Linda Grant has written:

Two-thirds of Europe's Jews didn't survive to put their imprint on history and those who did surely have a debt to the dead to repay: to bear witness and to make sure that, in their words, they create the next generation of witnesses.

The memory of this worst of tragedies must not be forgotten. It must not be repeated. We need to understand how human beings preserved their humanity when stripped of it or, in Primo Levi's great phrase, were drowned. [*Jewish Chronicle,* 12 December 1997, p. 25]

But for the first decade after the end of the war it seemed as if no one wanted either to know or to speak. The survivors had new lives to begin, the memories of traumas to be left behind as they traced loved ones, found new homes in other lands, married and raised children. [*Jewish Chronicle,* 12 December 1997, p. 25]

The evidence of the horrors had been glimpsed for a moment and the glimpse was enough. People everywhere wanted to look towards the future and they did not want to remember. They were very willing to know and yet not to know what had gone on so that life could 'return to normal'. The survivors sometimes promised themselves that they would remain silent, saying 'I'll never tell a living soul what happened to me' or perhaps 'No one would believe me if a told them what happened to me.' Often their children were to be protected from this knowing, for more than anything else they did not want their lives to be disturbed by the terrible histories they had known. They wanted them at least to have a chance to 'be normal'. If we were not to feel ungrateful, we had to learn to keep our own silence. We learnt to swallow our 'negative' feelings or to keep them firmly hidden.

Primo Levi's first book waited a decade to find a publisher. People were not ready to hear. Kitty Hart, in *Return to Auschwitz,* tells how she learnt not to speak about what happened to her, as she made a new life in post-war Britain. She learned not to share her memories in her family, and it could seem as if they were locked away, never to be retrieved.[7] But now, even the youngest of the survivors are in their sixties. The past comes back to haunt the fading generation of survivors and refugees. Sometimes they will speak to others, but they will still not speak to their own children. They might tell themselves, somewhat angrily, that their own children 'are not interested', but this might be because they have never really attempted to share themselves. It can be too painful for them to speak to their own children. They can still feel caught in the notion that controlled their relationships with their children since they could first speak, that their children will be damaged by these memories, though at some level the children already know. They have often had to carry unconsciously their parents' unresolved anger and violence. Sometimes they have been told 'what do you know about suffering', as if to invalidate their own entitlement to their emotions and feelings.[8]

Shaking the World

Bernard Offen was born in Krakow in 1929 and he survived the Shoah. His parents spoke Yiddish and he had to learn both Yiddish and Polish but he recalls that 'I was not allowed to be Polish because I was always called a Christ-killer, we Christ-killers.' His father was killed in Auschwitz and he still feels very sad whenever he thinks about him. He describes it thus: 'I made a bargain with G-d, when I was in Auschwitz, that – if I survive – I will witness. I was a boy of fourteen. So I'm keeping my word.' Describing his experience after the war, he does not think of himself as a victim any longer, although he recognizes that he is still suffering as a result of the experience. 'I was very, very angry at the whole world after the war a long, long, long time. And I had a dream: I was Atlas holding up the whole world. And I started to shake the thing, cursing everything else. I would be committing suicide I kept shaking the world, Because I'm part of the world, I shook myself awake from that dream.'

Bernard has come to believe that healing is possible, or at least that we can heal ourselves. Important for him in this process was a realization that 'if I had been born in Germany or in Austria I could have been on this side. I could have been this person. And that changed everything for me. We are in a creative process to connect with people.' But at the same time he recognizes that 'What is not possible to heal is the damage to the psyche. Not only to us as Jews but to the world . . . what horrors have been committed, all in the name of religion.' He is now involved in a 'Village-Project' looking for the names of people who might have once been members of the Izaak Synagogue in Kazimierz. He wants to recreate the village, to show a large piece of a small vanished community. As he is still exploring what he believes in and how to live his life, he has come to the recognition that 'I think the beginning for a healing world is the quality of relationship of two people; how two people are together, how I am with you and how you are with me. I am responsible for my own self'.

But if there is to be healing it will be a difficult process. There was a bitterness that many Polish Jews felt at the betrayals they felt so often at the hands of the Poles. Anna was often told in her family that 'the Poles were worse than the Germans', which was what also made the trip back to Poland so difficult for her. She had been told this so often that it was difficult to accept that there were also stories of Poles rescuing Jews. But it was the enthusiasm with which many Christian Poles joined in the humiliation of their once Jewish neighbours that left such deep scars because the Jews had lived alongside the Poles for a millennium and had regarded Poland as a home which they shared. This was what made it so painful. It seemed as if the Poles were too ready to help the Nazis with their anti-Semitic policies. It was not that they looked on as bystanders, refusing to come to the aid of the Jews, but that they actively participated in the humiliation of the Jews, that hurt so much.

Mordechai Gebirtig, who was born in Krakow in 1877, worked as a carpenter but he was also a well known poet and songwriter who was murdered in 1942 by the Germans. He wrote a poem entitled 'It Hurts':

> It hurts so bitterly
> Not to much the hatred
> burning inside the enemy.
> Not even the blow of the hands
> of a fierce foe;
> not the star of David
> on the arm.
> What a shame!
> For generations will there be
> shame on them.
> It hurts.
> It hurts bitterly
> that not the unknown enemy
> but them,
> the sons and daughters of Poland
> – their country will be ashamed one day –
> are laughing,
> a laughter gasping for breath
> when they see – as our common enemy
> is making a mockery of us
> in the streets,
> hitting old people, tormenting them,
> plundering unhindered,
> cutting off the beards of Jews
> as one cuts bread.
> And they !
> They have lost their land
> like us
> feeling the hand of the ferocious foe
> as we do,

laugh, cheer and laugh
at such a moment
when Poland's pride and honour
are disgraced.
When Poland's white eagle
is agonising on the floor
between beards
black and grey hair
from Jews' beards—
Isn't it a shame?
Aren't they spitting
into their own face?

It hurts
It hurts so bitterly!

This poem expresses anger but it also expressed a love and identification with Poland. It feels the hurt so intensely, partly because of the love. It expresses a deep and shocking sense of rejection and it refuses to identify these behaviours, however shocking, with Poland's white eagle. It is not the Jews that are bringing shame onto Poland. But at the same time it rejects the historical notion that the Poles could have not done otherwise, for they were equally the victims of Nazi brutality. This has been a post-war myth that has served to hide the shame of the willing participation of so many in the humiliation of the Jews. There is still an uneasy feeling when Jews are mentioned, as if people would prefer not to have to remember. But it is not always possible to forget, and the Jews were so much part of Poland's history and culture that their memory cannot so easily be erased. A new generation is asking its own questions and is refusing to be silenced. Young Poles want to understand what happened in the past, for at some level they recognize that they cannot make a different future until they have learned how to come to terms with their histories.

It is important to stress that it was not only in Poland that people stood by as Jews were publicly humiliated. My mother tells the story of how her brother, Herman, was caught wearing his best suit walking around Vienna. Soon after, Hitler's forces were welcomed in Vienna and the world seemed to change overnight for the Jews. He was made to clean the streets with a toothbrush as people looked on laughing. The crowds welcomed Hitler as his troops marched into Vienna and many of them were happy to play their part in the humiliation of the Jewish population. Suddenly the Jews were no longer their neighbours, nor could they count on the protection of citizenship.[9] The liberalism that so many identified with proved incapable of protecting them, as the rights they had taken for granted were withdrawn from them. Rather a liberal moral culture had somehow worked to undermine their resistance for it had fostered a false sense of security. It fostered a belief that they were guaranteed human dignity as the bearers of legal and political rights. It did not warn them that, if the state chose to withdraw these rights, then they would be left bereft of the cultural sources of human dignity. They would be seen as 'less than human'. It was the ease with which this could be carried through that remains the challenge, still unanswered, to liberal moral and political theory.

Often Jews felt abandoned and alone, as if they were to be regarded as 'dispensable' within the West. They had made notable contributions to the societies they identified with and they had often readily paid the price of citizenship, even when this meant renouncing their Jewishness as a public identity. They were often ready to assimilate into the dominant cultures and treat their Jewishness as a matter of individual religious belief alone. In Germany they possibly felt most assimilated and 'like everyone else' and were often very identified with German literature, music, and culture. This is why it became so difficult to 'take in' what was happening to them and the painful exclusions from civil society. They were convinced that it 'would not last' because they believed they lived in the civilized heart of Europe where these things 'just do not happen'. Sometimes Jews felt that they would be protected by their bourgeois status, but in the end this was not to help them. But it did help many to escape before it was too late, and paradoxically it was the German Jewish community that survived in larger numbers.[10]

Addressing Holocaust victims, Jewish leaders and French Cabinet ministers, French President Jacques Chirac handed over files containing the names of all the Jews arrested and deported during the Second World War to a Jewish documentation centre in Paris. These handwritten files were discovered five years ago in a French ministry archive by Nazi-hunter Serge Klarsfeld. Chirac called these files 'testimony to the moral abdication of a state'. In 1995, he became the first French leader to acknowledge France's role in the persecution of the Jews during the Vichy era. He had broken with the post-war French consensus that Vichy was an aberration that did not represent or reflect France as a whole. The Jews knew a different reality from their wartime experience but this was to be silenced and ignored by successive post-war French governments. France was to turn its back on its own history and teach its children a different story. This is why it was so important to hear Chirac say that

France had to recognize that 'arrests and raids (against Jews) were organised with the help of the French administration. Confinement and transit camps – like Pithiviers, Beaune-La-Rolands, Drancy and Compiegne – were under the responsibility of the French administration' (*Jewish Chronicle,* 12 December 1997, p. 6).

President Chirac added that France's attempts to come to terms with the past had been 'too long postponed'. Coming in the wake of the announcements by the French Church, these are welcome developments. We can welcome them whilst still wanting to understand why they have taken so long. It was easier for people to console themselves with stories of the French resistance than to accept the painful realities of collusion. It was easier for people to renounce the Vichy state as if it were not French and to make the Vichy state responsible for the crimes of 1940 to 1944. It took many years before France was ready to hear about the darker history of collaboration and to face up to the ways that the French had colluded in the treatment of their own Jewish citizens. Often it is easier to split from the past than to face the reality of what went on. The Jews were not protected by the noble republican traditions. They were also aware of what happened to Dreyfus and the difficult years that were needed to clear his name. This is part of a history of anti-Semitism that people still have to find ways of coming to terms with, rather than learning to treat it as an aberration that has nothing to do with French history and culture.

Recently Switzerland has also had to come to terms with its collusions as a banker to the Nazi regime. Somehow Switzerland had been able to trade on its neutrality and, as children growing up in the 1950s, we learned little about its involvement in the war. As far as we were concerned it had escaped with its moral standing intact. But the recent revelations to do with Nazi gold tell a very different story and we learned just how deeply complicit the Swiss banking system was in financing the Nazi regime. The Swiss banks profited directly from the Holocaust and from the activities of the Nazi war machine, and they often refused to cooperate with survivors who had little documentation to support their claims. This was a shameful history that was long hidden. 30,000 Jews were granted refuge in Switzerland during the war but the country turned away a similar number to an almost certain death.

In 1940, Yitzhak Mayer who was later to become Israeli ambassador to Switzerland was only five. He joined his mother and father on a crowded train in Antwerp hoping to escape Nazi terror. They made it to France but his father was arrested there and deported to his death in Auschwitz. Young Yitzhak, and his brother and mother, managed to survive and headed for refuge in Switzerland. They reached the border in the middle of the night and were stopped by Swiss officials. He recalled: 'There was no wire fence on the border. Just a street, German soldiers and death on one side. Life on the other.' The Swiss officials initially said that they could not enter the country. But a doctor was called and he ruled that his mother was too sick to be deported and needed hospital treatment. That insistence saved them. His family was given accommodation with a Jewish woman in Eglislaw, a village near Zurich, and he went to the local school. He remembers it as a time when he was 'loved and cared for and treated like a human being'. Schoolmate Verena Stettler said : 'He was not like us because he had another culture, another language and we admired him because of that' (*Jewish Chronicle,* 12 December 1977, p. 2).

Yitzhak Meyer, 63 in late 1997, returned to Egislau with a message that, despite international criticism, the Swiss also had some reason to be proud of their behaviour during the war. Remembering his time as a frightened refugee from Nazi terror he declared at an emotional reception in the village that 'I am a voice of the saved souls', and said that 'For the rest of my life I will feel deep gratitude for Egislau and Switzerland.' Thinking back over the years he said that 'Now I am a father (of three daughters) and grandfather (of two). The person who saved me, saved six lives. Those who would have sent me to the other side of the street on the border would have killed six people' (*Jewish Chronicle,* 12 December 1977, p. 2).

Facing History

Only recently has it been possible to face up to the time of Nazi occupation in Poland and to write openly about what went on. The whole subject of the extermination of the Jews has been dealt with according to an official line that has rarely been questioned – that a large majority of Poles sympathized with the Jews and helped and saved them where they could. The sporadic incidents of blackmail and informing and of Jews being handed over to the Germans were isolated cases dealt with harshly by the underground. Rafael Scharf in his recently collected essays *Poland, What Have I to do with Thee* . . . thinks about these issues differently.[11] In a 1984 lecture to an international conference at Oxford on Polish–Jewish relations he recognized that both sides approach it with a heavy heart. Many Jews do not want to return to a chapter in their painful history that they consider closed. They do not want to open up old wounds but prefer to forget about the past in Poland, turn their backs on it forever.

I believe that Poles who want to talk and think about these matters (maybe only a handful of them), feel somewhat ill at ease with the subject, as if expecting that something will come up that they will find difficult to cope with. No one likes to be censured, least of all justly. [Rafael Scharf, 'Cum ira et studio' in *Poland, What Have I to do with Thee?* (Krakow, Foundation Judaica, 1996), p. 247]

At the same time Sharf recognizes that, for the Poles, it is a subject of primary importance. As he expresses it

A millennium of Jewish presence on Polish lands and their sudden and final absence, are facts without which Poles are not able to understand their past and, therefore, their present . . . Moral regeneration calls for an authentic dialogue with the past . . . In the case of Poles gaining self-knowledge, the Jews appear as a witness who must be listened to carefully and who can, of course be questioned. [Rafael Scharf, 'Cum ira et studio' in *Poland, What Have I to do with Thee?* (Krakow, Foundation Judaica, 1996), p. 248]

For the Jews who lived through the occupation the official line is contrary to their experience

that the Poles, with a few exceptions – for them great and eternal praise – did not show any sympathy, did not help or save, that a Jew in hiding or in disguise lived in fear not so much of the Germans but of his neighbours or passers-by, with their acute Polish sensitivity for Jewish features, manner of speaking or fear in their eyes. If the Jews could have depended not on active help, which called for heroism, but neutrality, causing the Pole to look the other way- the chances of survival would have increased a hundredfold. [Rafael Scharf, 'Cum ira et studio' in *Poland, What Have I to do with Thee?* (Krakow, Foundation Judaica, 1996), p. 250]

Rafael Sharf considers a report written by Jan Karski who was the first person to bring to the West an authentic account of the gas chambers and crematoria. In his report for Stanislaw Kot, the Minister of Home Affairs in exile, he declares that as was the case in inter-war Poland, many Poles are hostile to the Jews and in principle sympathize with the objectives of the Germans to 'solve' the Jewish question in the occupied territories. Here is an excerpt:

The solution of the 'Jewish Question' by the Germans – I must state this with a full sense of responsibility for what I am saying – represents a very dangerous tool in the hands of the Germans, leading toward the 'moral pacification' of a broad section of Polish society . . . Although the nation loathes them (the Germans) mortally, this question creates a narrow bridge, upon which the

Germans and a large part of Polish society find themselves in agreement . . .
[Jan Karski, quoted in Rafael Scharf, 'Cum ira et studio' in *Poland, What
Have I to do with Thee?* (Krakow, Foundation Judaica, 1996), p. 251]

If the extent and persistence of anti-Semitism among the Polish population, even during the war against Hitler, became public knowledge, this
could discredit Poland's cause in the eyes of the Allies. Another version
of the report was prepared that portrayed the Polish population as united
in their condemnation against German anti-Jewish activities. The truth
of what was going on was to be covered over. But Sharf is clear in his
view that

> The fact that the gassing and burning of Jews, which went on for years, was
> never interrupted by a single external act of blind rage has strengthened my
> conviction that the Poles, although they may have observed it all with
> compassion, do not feel sufficiently moved and enraged to intervene individ-
> ually or collectively, with 'their bare teeth' or by whatever means, regardless
> of consequences. What the Germans did in the death-camps could only have
> been done to the Jews. [Rafael Scharf, 'Cum ira et studio' in *Poland, What
> Have I to do with Thee?* (Krakow, Foundation Judaica, 1996), p. 251]

At the same time Scharf acknowledges that, in their bitterness, Jews have
often been insensitive to the predicament and sufferings of the Poles:

> They do not remember that attempts to help a Jew threatened death; they tend
> to think that the attitude to Jewry is the only important matter, to the exclusion
> of all other matters; they brood over the dark side of things, because, as the
> poet says, 'wrong is engraved in stone, and kindness in sand.' [Rafael Scharf,
> 'Cum ira et studio' in *Poland, What Have I to do with Thee?* (Krakow,
> Foundation Judaica, 1996), p. 251]

But as Scharf recognizes

> It is a tragedy of the Poles that in the midst of the cruel visitation of fate, they
> were exposed to an unprecedented moral trial. They did not come through it
> victorious. It can be argued that nobody would have come through it any
> better, but that is little comfort for the Jews. [Rafael Scharf, *Poland, What
> Have I to do with Thee?* (Krakow, Foundation Judaica, 1996), p.252]

Forgetfulness

When the war ended it was easy for the world to move on, but it was not
so easy for the Jewish people who had lost so much with the destruction
of European Jewry. Anna's mother returned to her town only to be warned

that there was no place for her. She had to leave. The murder of survivors at Kielce was a reminder of a continuing Polish anti-Semitism. It seemed as if little had been learned. Many Poles wanted to turn their backs on all things Jewish, as if nothing of any consequence had happened. As Scharf expresses it

> A shroud of forgetfulness was thrown over this awesome breach in society's fabric. People tried hard not to notice this great absence (although the Jews recruited for the Department of Security were scrupulously counted). Even in Auschwitz, for years, the Jews were passed over in silence. 'Babi Yar' – style. Information on the Jewish section could only be obtained by persistent questioning, and then the key had to be searched for. All this was supposedly in line with the principle that although only Jews were gassed and incinerated and many more of them died than all the others put together, no distinction should be made among the victims according to nationality. [Rafael Scharf, 'Cum ira et studio' in *Poland, What Have I to do with Thee?* (Krakow, Foundation Judaica, 1996), p. 253]

As Sartre recognizes in *Anti-Semite and Jew* (New York, Shocken Books, 1960), this erasure of Jewishness was also written into an Enlightenment vision of modernity. This was an aspect of modernity that Marx failed to question when he wrote 'On the Jewish Question'. I have attempted to think through some of the implications of this in *Recovering the Self* because it fosters a particular modern form of intolerance. Liberal freedom lies in splitting from a Jewish tradition and culture that is defined as 'backward' and in Kantian terms as a form of 'unfreedom' and 'determination'. Here we meet the silencing of Jewish experience and culture within an orthodox state Marxism. There is to be no recognition of the particularities of a Jewish history, however tragic. Rather it is to be subsumed into a narrative of the nation, as if Jews were only allowed to become 'Poles' in their death. The recognition that was to be denied to them in their lives when in pre-war Poland they were constantly to be reminded that they were Jews and therefore could not be Poles, was somehow to claim them in their deaths.

Wanting to reclaim the period of independence that Poland knew after the First World War as integral to a new self conception with the end of communist rule, it becomes difficult to acknowledge the strength of anti-Semitism for this compromises the vision post-communist Poland wants to have of its past as an independent state. Anti-Semitism grew in strength during this period and political parties had, as part of their programmes, a more-or-less brutal battle against their fellow Jewish citizens. As Scharf recalls, an anti-Jewish movement grew in strength and came to be for us an ever-present force, filling the atmosphere like ether. The fact that the Poles were and are not aware of this – at least this is what many claim – is for us hard to believe and understand . . . Was it a figment of our imagination that there was an officially approved boycott, discrimination in all areas of state service, daily incitement in the press, the programmatic and primitive anti-Judaism of the Church, sporadic pogroms. In universities, in some faculties, there was a numerus clausus and, often, 'ghetto-benches'. (Maria Dabrowska called it 'the annual shame' – it is good to remember her for this.) [Rafael Scharf, 'Cum ira et studio' in *Poland, What Have I to do with Thee?* (Krakow, Foundation Judaica, 1996), p. 249]

Scharf also responds to someone who had asked, very pertinently, if it was so bad why was it so good? Despite the fact that the climate was so severe and maybe thanks to it, a specific Jewish civilization flourished. As Scharf puts it:

on these lands there blossomed a full, rich, varied and creative Jewish life. There was total freedom of worship, an autonomy in religious matters, . . . there were schools where instruction was held in Hebrew and Yeshivoth for Talmudic studies; there were newspapers printed in Polish, Yiddish and Hebrew . . . There were political parties – Zionist, religious, workers, assimilationist; . . . theatres, charitable and educational associations, sports clubs. [Rafael Scharf, 'Cum ira et studio' in *Poland, What Have I to do with Thee?* (Krakow, Foundation Judaica, 1996), p. 249]

In a piece that Scharf wrote for the opening of The Centre of Jewish Culture, in Kazimierz, Krakow, 24 November 1993, 'As in a dream', he warns us against the loss of those forms and values that were the essence of Jewish life in the Diaspora, and points to a shared feeling, despite the diversity of Jewish life in Poland. As he puts it:

One of its hallmarks was the conviction that – irrespective of the poor living conditions and daily struggles – man must aspire to things above the mundane, strive for a realisation of some high ideal, however defined. There was a deeply ingrained perception that decent behaviour towards fellow human beings, religious practice, the observance of ethical norms, respect for the scholar, pursuit of learning would speed the Messiah on his way and would initiate an era of universal justice. [Rafael Scharf, 'As in a dream' in *Poland, What Have I to do with Thee?* (Krakow, Foundation Judaica, 1996), p. 265]

After the war many Poles wanted to forget what had existed before. This was often a wilful forgetting for they did not want to be reminded of their neighbours who were no longer alive, or the people who use to live in the houses they now claimed as their own.[12] But the walls carry their own memories and objects do not forget. However hard we try to erase the histories that objects carry, they can serve as reminders of what we would rather choose to suppress. It is not just that others might remind us of who lived in these houses before, but as Freud recognizes, what we repress often returns in our dreams to haunt us. This is not only to do with individual memory, but with collective memories too. There comes a time when it feels easier to face the past, for this seems the only way we can begin to lay it to rest. But in the years after the war, as Scharf reminds us

> There was a wide-spread feeling of relief among the Poles, that the 'Jewish problem' had been 'solved' in a manner for which they could not be blamed, and that Poland could now be rebuilt without the Jews - and all the better for it. The Jewish survivors who came out of the camps and hiding places often heard the opinion, that like or not, Hitler had done a good job on the Jews. Hitler's lesson – as Karski foresaw – found adept pupils. [Rafael Scharf, 'As in a dream' in *Poland, What Have I to do with Thee?* (Krakow, Foundation Judaica, 1996), p. 253]

The few who survived due to their possessing 'Aryan documents' (documents proving that they were not Jews but Aryans) realized that it was safer to continue the masquerade in the existing climate. Often they did not betray their real identity, even to their children. Those returning from Russia also learned to assume some sort of protective cover. They thought they would get by but their origins had been duly marked in their files and even the most loyal of Communist Party members, who had willingly forsaken any connection with their Jewish past, found that they were to be exposed in 1967 when the authorities again sought to regain popularity by unleashing a wave of anti-Semitism. For many Jews it was the final signal that, even if they wanted to leave their Jewishness behind, the communist authorities would not let them. Many Jews were forced to leave knowing that Poland had no place for them. They carried a deeply embedded feeling of having been wronged and some felt embittered because of the trust they had put in the new communist state.

Scharf wonders 'how far the Poles are aware of the fact that with the Jews an authentic part of *their* Poland was obliterated'. Was it the Jews alone who were to suffer the 'trauma of unreciprocated love'? Speaking for the many Jews of his generation, the last generation of Jews who can remember pre-war Poland, he acknowledged that they cannot erase from their hearts this country where 'they were born and grew up,' where – as Tuwin wrote – 'in Polish they confessed the disquiet of their first love and in Polish they stammered of its rapture and tempests'; where they loved the landscape, the language, the poetry; where they were ready to shed their blood for Poland and be her true sons, that this was, evidently, not enough leaves them broken-hearted. [Rafael Scharf, 'As in a dream' in *Poland, What Have I to do with Thee?* (Krakow, Foundation Judaica, 1996), p. 254.]

Notes

1. For a crucial introduction to the writings of Maimonides, a central figure in Jewish philosophy, see Moses Maimonides, *The Guide of the Perplexed* translated with notes by Shlomo Pines (Chicago, University of Chicago Press, 1963). A helpful introduction, which places Maimonides in historical and cultural context, is provided by David Hartman as *Maimonides: Torah and Philosophical Quest* (Philadelphia, Jewish Publication Society, 1976).
2. I have explored Kant's relationship to an Enlightenment vision of modernity and the implications that Kantian ethics has for a sense of history and culture, in Victor Seidler, *Kant, Respect and Injustice: The Limits of Liberal Moral Theory* (London, Routledge, 1986).
3. The image of angels appears throughout Walter Benjamin's work. In the early 1920s he had wanted to found a journal that would have been called *Angelus Novus*.
4. For a discussion of notions of progress in their relationship to modernity, see for example, Peter Berger, *Facing Up to Modernity* (London, Penguin, 1979); Alasdair MacIntyre, *After Virtue* (London, Duckworth, 1981) and *Against The Self-Images of the Age* (London, Duckworth, 1971) and Daniel Bell, *The Cultural Contradictions of Capitalism* (New York, Basic Books, 1976).
5. For an introduction to the ideas and historical context of Moses Mendelssohn see A.Altman, *Moses Mendelssohn* (London, Routledge, 1978) A more generalized account of Judaism's relationship to modernity is provided by David Biale, *Power And Powerlessness In Jewish History* (New York, Basic Books, 1986). For a more specific German context see, David Sorkin, *The Transformation of German Jewry*, 1780–1840 (New York, 1987).
6. For a historical exploration of the ways Jews responded to the French Enlightenment, see Arthur Herzberg, *The French Enlightenment and*

the Jews (New York, Schocken Books, 1968), Leon Poliakov, *The Aryan Myth* (London, Sussex University Press, 1974) and Leon Poliakov, *The History of Anti-Semitism* (Oxford, OUP, 1990).

7. Kitty Hart, in *Return to Auschwitz* (Manchester, Granada Books) shares how it was only when her children had grown up and people at worked asked her about herself, that she began to share her history and appreciate that it was something that 'could be talked about'. Tony Kushner in a paper 'Survivors on the 1940s and beyond' given to the Wiener Library Conference 'Family/History: Survivors, Refugees and Their children', held in London on 29 January 1995 suggested that since the little treatment that was given to concentration camps in the 1950s and 1960s focused on the sexual maltreatment of women, it is hardly surprising that many survivors were reluctant to talk of their experience.

8. For an understanding of some of the psychotherpeutic work that has been done with survivors and their children see Aaron Hass, *The Aftermath: Living with the Holocaust* (Cambridge, CUP, 1995); Helen Epstein, *Children of the Holocaust: Conversations with Sons and Daughters of Survivors* (New York, G.P. Putnam, 1979) and Dan Bar-On, *Fear and Hope: Three Generations of the Holocaust* (Cambridge, Harvard University Press, 1995).

9. For a historical account of the experience of Jews within Vienna which helps to explain the centrality of Jewishness and anti-Semitism in the evolution of nineteenth-century Austro German politics and culture, Robert S. Wistrich, *The Jews of Vienna in the Age of Franz Joseph* (London, Vallentine Mitchell/Litman Library, 1989).

10. An illuminating account of the experience of German Jewry in the years of Nazi rule, written partly as an account of the life and work of Leo Baeck, is Leonard Baker, *Days of Sorrow and Pain: Leo Baeck and the Berlin Jews* (New York, OUP, 1978).

11. Rafael F. Scharf was born in Krakow in 1914 and obtained a degree in law from the Jagiellonian University in Krakow before emigrating to England. His writings have been collected as *Poland, What Have I to do with Thee . . .* (Krakow, Foundation Judaica and Drukarnia Uniwersytetu Jagiellonskiego, 1996).

12. For an account of the recent discussions that have taken place in Poland about the Holocaust and the fate of Polish Jewry, see Antony Polonsky (ed.), *My Brother's Keeper: Recent Polish debates on the Holocaust* (London, Routledge, 1990). See also Zygmunt Bauman 'The Homecoming of Unwelcome Strangers: Eastern European Jewry Fifty Years after the War' *Jewish Quarterly*, no. 135, Autumn 1989.

7

Even If We Were All Wise . . .

Learning

We are nearing a time when there will not be a single eye-witness of the Shoah, no one who themselves went through the inferno, there will no longer be survivors from the camps or those who whose salvation proved to be exile in Siberia. Rafael Scharf believes that then the historical perspective and the parameters of these issues will change. Then it will be less about how Poles and Jews lived with each other but something bigger and more universal. As Scharf puts it:

> What is at issue here is a great, common cause of universal significance. The extermination of the Jews on Polish territory was a crucial event in history, marking the crisis of Christianity and the crisis of our civilisation (some people regard these concepts as synonymous, but fortunately that is not so). Those events cannot be forgotten or ignored, they will weigh upon future generations for all time. [Rafael Scharf, in *Poland, What Have I to do with Thee?* (Krakow, Foundation Judaica, 1996), p. 258]

In an essay 'Let us Talk . . .' Rafael Scharf, asks about the lessons that human beings will draw from the Shoah. He frames questions that remain inescapable if we are to think about the relationship of the Holocaust to modernity and not to treat it as some kind of aberration which lies somehow outside and beyond history.[1]

> How will they face up to it, conscious of the enormity of the evil which they are capable of perpetrating? How will they renew their faith in the basic moral values in a world of which, in Adorno's words, 'we cannot be too much afraid' and where there exist instruments of destruction which put even the gas chambers in shadow? On answers to these questions hang all our tomorrows. [Rafael Scharf, 'Let us talk . . .' in *Poland, What Have I to do with Thee?* (Krakow, Foundation Judaica, 1996), p. 258]

These questions press on our todays, let alone our tomorrows. They help me recognize some of the fear that feels much closer to the surface of everyday life than it did when I was young. It also helps name a particular insecurity, a not knowing when the knock on the door, as Bonhoffer put it, will be for me.

To those who say that there can be little to add to the painful history of Polish–Jewish relations, Scharf answers with a sentence from the *Hagada*, which is the story that Jews read together on Passover/Pesach: *Afim kulanu hakhamin* . . . ('Even if we were all wise . . .') which in free translation can be taken to mean that although we have learned from many sources and have absorbed a great deal of wisdom, nonetheless it is incumbent upon us to tell this story . . . This is a story that many Polish Jews refused to tell to their children for they wanted them to live a different life and they did not want to burden them with the pain they carried themselves. My father died before he could have really shared his stories with me, although I do not know whether he ever would have done so. There was too much pain tied up with Warsaw, where his brothers had been murdered as well as his sisters in law and nieces and nephews. He was the only person from his family to survive and he did not live long with this knowledge.

This makes me all the more grateful for the stories that Rafael Scharf shares for in many ways I feel that he is giving me back a sense of my own history and so part of myself. I was given his book, *Poland, What Have I To Do With Thee* as a 52nd birthday present a few weeks after we arrived home from our own trip to Poland. It was a wonderful gift and I have been carrying it around, as one does with one's own books when they have just been published. I wanted to be near it, and I have been reading it slowly because it has so much to say to me and for me. I respected Scharf's refusal to heed the words of those who said 'why bother with these painful matters, what good will it do?' I share his sense that it would be an 'impoverishment' to turn away from these 'difficult' questions and his suspicion that those who would distance themselves from them would also distance themselves from other serious topics as well.

Rafael Scharf explains his position clearly.

> I believe that the more things concern us the better. Surely there is plenty to talk about; our history – the part which is common and the part which is separate; about how things really went between us, at close quarters and at a distance . . . about that which united and that which divided us, about all that, as long as it is not superficial but serious and with concern for the truth. This does not mean that we shall see the truth in the same way, because the truth is complicated and has many dimensions; we are sensitive to some of its aspects, blind to others; only some segments of it are accessible to each of us. The

sheer step that this is so seems to be a step in the right direction. [Rafael Scharf, 'Let us talk . . .' in *Poland, What Have I to do with Thee?* (Krakow, Foundation Judaica, 1996), p. 259]

For Jews whose families lived in Poland these memories and explorations have a special meaning, for it is to share a history they have often learned to discount. It is easy to feel that this has significance for our parents, but it can have little meaning for the second generation that was born in different lands. What does it mean to assume aspects of an identity that I seem to have lived without for so long? Is this mere nostalgia for a lost past or does it help to repair and bring together pieces that did not seem to fit together too well? Does it promise a way of recognizing why I might feel different in the present and what might still strike me as 'hollow' in the identities I have created for myself? Can it help rethink the fragmentation of post-modern identities through helping us rethink the nature of a particular form of diaspora identity?[2] It might be tempting to feel, in postmodern terms, that if this history carries no particular significance for me in the present, then it can be safely left behind. It might be of 'historical' interest but that this is a separate matter.

Is there is a particular responsibility for Jews with a Polish background to remember so that we can keep alive a vision of community and tradition for the present? This is not to recreate a past that was brutally murdered, but it is to honour values and relationships that might have something to teach us in the present. It means questioning the silence of our parents, possibly looking for lessons that were too painful for them to teach. But this is not to blame them or to urge them to change decisions they have made for themselves, for this is to learn for ourselves and possibly learn something of value that we can also pass onto our children. As Rafael Scharf shares his particular sense of responsibility he declares

We, who form a link in the chain of the 1000 years of Jewish presence on Polish soil, does it not behove us to remember that part of our heritage is to cultivate it and pass it on? Every brick, every stone, every graveyard, every footprint, each document, each scrap of paper, each trace in whatever form, is valuable beyond measure for a nation whose roots give sense to its history and whose memory of the past vouchsafes the continuity of its existence. The history of the Jews did not begin in 1948 with the creation of the State of Israel. A large part of the history was enacted on Polish lands. Should one, could one, turn one's back on it, bury it, forget it? Surely not, surely the very opposite must be the case. [Rafael Scharf, 'Let us talk . . .' in *Poland, What Have I to do with Thee?* (Krakow, Foundation Judaica, 1996), p. 259]

Jewish Memory

Many Jews who left Poland specifically decided to turn their backs on their history there and to begin life anew. They did not want to take their memories with them or pass them onto their children. Often those lucky enough to escape wanted their children not to be burdened by a painful past that could so easy crush them. Rather they wanted their children to become 'English' or 'American' for this is where security and safety seemed to rest. A sense of history seemed to stand in the way of a vision that was looking towards the future. At some level it feared the past, for it was easy to feel that 'nothing good had come of it' and that it had the power to contaminate the present. Young Jews growing up in the shadows of the Shoah were often not told about the terrible experiences their parents had gone through. Often parents felt that they somehow owed it to their children to carry this particular burden for themselves. But of course they passed it on silently and unconsciously, but this often made it difficult for the second generation to name the burdens we carry or to name the sense of fraught difference we felt from our peers, both Jewish and non-Jewish. We felt different, but often we did not know why.

But if our parents did not want to remember their lives in Poland or in Austria or in Germany but learned to put them aside, how were we supposed to remember as children? It seemed as if there was a gap that could not be breached, a separation of different worlds that could not communicate with each other. Often children learned not to ask their parents too any questions for they had learnt that they 'had suffered enough'. We learnt to be proud of our Jewish heritage but this was often set within Biblical terms and was not given a grounding within, for instance, the history of Poland. Rather, as children, we learned to identify with Israel as presenting a different, more hopeful vision of the future (without, it must be said, learning what we also needed to know about the Palestinians and their lands). But Zionism, which brought about the state of Israel, was, as Scharf recognizes, in its basic assumptions, a protest against the life in the diaspora. It meant that 'its side-effects, intended and accidental, was the irrevocable loss of those forms and values which were the essence of Jewish life in the Diaspora'. [Rafael Scharf, 'As in a dream' in *Poland, What Have I to do with Thee?* (Krakow, Foundation Judaica, 1996), p. 265]

This created its own form of double consciousness within the diaspora for, as young children growing up in the shadows of the Holocaust, we found ourselves with a split vision, in which the Eastern European diaspora was linked with 'weakness' and with 'shame' for, to repeat, they had supposedly gone 'like lambs to the slaughter'. We did not learn enough about the different forms of resistance, both military and spiritual and about the dignity people sustained through terrible times. Little was spoken about and we had to make sense of the terrible images that were shown on the television in the 1950s.[3] We absorbed these realities with our eyes, but still there was little explanation Few of us were lucky enough to hear a Rafael Scharf who could declare so openly

> I love that Jewish Poland which is no more. I love it with a love which is different from the one I nurture for the State of Israel . . . I see and feel that it was a world of authentic, uniquely Jewish experience – in a sense in which this is not recreated in a normal country like Israel. [Rafael Scharf, 'As in a dream' in *Poland, What Have I to do with Thee?* (Krakow, Foundation Judaica, 1996), p. 265]

This is paradoxical for many, like Isaiah Berlin, who felt that Israel remained a necessity because of the persecution Jews suffered and because it provided a necessary space in which they did not have to accommodate or worry that the actions of other Jews would automatically be thought to reflect upon them. But rather than being in contradiction, it offeres a different truith that also needs to be recognized.

The diaspora has its own memories but it is not simply a matter of learning to live between two spaces, learning to appreciate what one is learning from each, and bringing them together in some kind of hybrid identity. Often it is very difficult to bring different cultural memories into relation with each other and uneasy choices have to be made. Memories could carry too much pain and the survivors and refugees often needed to put these memories aside, so that they could offer their children the chance for a more 'normal' life. John Lemberger who is the executive director of Amcha – Hebrew for 'your people' – which offers psychological support for Holocaust survivors and their heirs recognizes how the unresolved issues of money and assets were a source of anxiety and reminder of the world's reaction to the plight of the Jews before, during, and after the Holocaust. As he explains it: 'After the war many survivors put their traumas deep inside them and went on rebuilding their lives. They didn't forget, but they put (the past) out of their sight and out of their minds for 50 years' (*Jewish Chronicle,* 5 December 1997, p. 3).

Many of the survivors have now retired and it was common for them to associate lack of work with lack of worth – and even death – because the Nazis immediately killed anyone who was unable to work. Levember writes: 'As they get older, they naturally confront their own mortality, and questions of why they survived while other loved ones perished also begin to resurface' (p. 3). As memories return, so do these difficult questions that refuse to be settled. Even then these questions are often not asked directly, but they hang uneasily around the silences in the family. Sometimes these anxieties are passed into the emotional bodies of the next generation who can feel an added urgency to 'make good' in their lives, so redeeming not only themselves, but their parents too. Sometimes it is the 'success' that the children achieve that is supposed to 'account', in terms of some emotional justice, for the survival of the parents. Often this can be experienced as an unnamed sense of pressure that is difficult to locate, but is no less demanding for being unnamed.

Survival

As survivors and refugees split from their painful memories of the past, they often refused to share their memories with their children. They often wanted to stress the 'positive' in the present and refused to listen to anything else. For decades after the war, analysts did not connect the parents' Holocaust experience with the children's lives. Although many survivors and their children were analysed at Anna Freud's Hampstead clinic the specialized index didn't include the item 'survivor', let alone 'survivor's child'. Only in 1966 did a Canadian psychiatrist, Vivien Rakoff, notice that he was seeing more adolescents whose parents were Holocaust survivors than he would have expected. Reports suggested that children of survivors were exploding with the aggression, which their parents had suppressed, and that many were depressed and suffered from a symbiotic relationship with their mothers, which hindered their separation. Aaron Hass in *In the Shadow of the Holocaust* (I. B. Taurus, 1991 p 57) argues that survivor parents tend to over-invest in their children and over-protect them. One child recalled 'We were continually fed, burped, stroked, tweaked, and fondled until we were well into our thirties' (p. 57).

After such overwhelming losses, all separations to the survivors can feel like loss. Parents can find it difficult to encourage their children's autonomy and individuation and can experience signs of separation as a threat. To the child, separation can also invoke fears of annihilation and, as Harvey and Carol Baracos reported (Harvey A. Baracos and Carol B. Baracos 'Separation – Individuation Conflicts in Children of Holocaust Survivors', *Journal of Contemporary Psychotherapy*, vol 11, no. 1, Spring/ Summer 1980) they can feel considerable guilt at wanting to be different from their parents. Even if they find their parents' constant vigilance overcontrolling and interfering, they often reluctantly yield to it because they often experience their parents' anxieties as their own. Anne Karpf in her illuminating study *The War After* (London, Minerva, 1997) reports studies that show a reversal of roles, a parenting of the parents, with the child comforting the adult rather than the other way round.[4] Somehow this links to the high expectations parents have for their children, as if whatever they do cannot be enough. A Holocaust survivor might exclaim, 'For this I survived the Nazis? For this I survived the camps?' inducing wholesale guilt in their children. Helen Epstein in her pioneering work *Children of the Holocaust* also suggests that parents often found it difficult to tolerate the merest unhappiness in their offspring: 'If they were to see me unhappy or unhealthy, they would feel punished and I didn't want to punish them' (p. 307).

Mourning was seen as a problem for many survivors. Anne Karpf reports work by Krystal and Niederland that argues that 'not only did the survivors have no opportunity to mourn their losses during the Holocaust, but that after the war their guilt at having survived prevented them from completing the work of mourning' (p. 226). She helpfully questions a simplistic notion of survivor guilt that became so prevalent that therapists sometimes suggested to survivors, according to Karpf, that 'You must feel guilty for having survived when all around you died', as if guilt could be assumed and the survivor had indeed committed a crime. She helpfully clarifies when she acknowledged that 'Certainly some survivors did forcefully express a sense of guilt and shame at having lived: as Primo Levi put it, "The 'saved' of the Lager were not the best, those predestined to do good . . . The worst survived – that is, the fittest; the best all died"' (*The Drowned and the Saved,* (London, Abacus, 1989), pp. 62–3). The task of mourning in such circumstances is, however, fare more complex than the crude early formulations allowed. For example, many survivors felt, as an Israeli analyst (Rafael Moses) put, that 'if one mourns *too* well, one betrays the dead' (p. 227). The Freudian concept of mourning might itself be inappropriate; as one survivor puts it: 'It's too many to mourn' (p. 227).[5]

But often unresolved feelings were passed to the second generation. Reports often detected an extreme identification with the lives of the first generation. Again Ann Karpf provides a helpful setting bringing together recent research by Aaron Hass, Judith Kestenberg and other:

> In a process labelled 'transposition', survivors children were described as living simultaneously in the present and in the past, transposing themselves to their parents' past, and attempting to compensate for their parents' losses. Sometimes

they tested their body endurance, and their ability to survive being in hiding . . .
In institutional settings, they reacted as if their very survival was at stake,
while in other settings they behaved as if every decision was a matter of life
and death. Illness was omnipresent: 'Every time my throat hurt, my mother
was sure that I had cancer'. Another child of survivors recalled that 'Everything
was life and death. They were always waiting for the worst to happen' [Ann
Karpf, *The War After* (London, Minerva, 1997)]

The way in which the past resonates in the present is linked to memory
and the ways in which we understand identities. Many Jews found it
difficult to develop a positive sense of Jewish identity because they
unconsciously associated being Jewish with being killed.[6]

There was also an ambivalence because parents wanted their children
to settle comfortably into the gentile society they inhabited, but they also
wanted them to remember the culture and families that they had lost. A
liberal moral culture encouraged many Jewish people to erase their
Jewishness, assuming that it was a matter of individual religious belief
alone, so that if you had rationally questioned religious faith, this meant
that you could chose to construct a post-modern identity in terms of your
own chosing.[7] This sustained the Kantian notion that history and culture
were forms of unfreedom and determination that could be forsaken/erased
as you moved towards individual freedom and autonomy. Sometimes this
goes hand-in-hand with a rejection of Freud and psychotherapy as
essentially 'reductive', which often means that we do not have to come
to terms with emotional and cultural histories. Often it is with small
children that these unresolved issues begin to return as they ask the
questions we have so often avoided for ourselves. They want to know
about their grandparents, even if we have left this knowledge behind.

A more differentiated and complex understanding of survival has
slowly developed, where Holocaust survivors are no longer conceptualized
as a homogenous group. Researchers show more awareness of pre-camp
personalities and experiences as well as differences between camps and
different people's experience within the same camp. They have begun to
appreciate the importance of having survived in a group or at least as
one of a pair. Widening their gaze from the wartime traumas they have
also begun to appreciate the traumatic experience of immigration, of
losing their homeland and mother tongue, as well as the age and stage in
the lifecycle when such losses were experienced, where the trauma also
has to do with the early separation from parents.

It is also being recognized that the second generation also carries these
experiences differentially. Sometimes it is the oldest child who has to

carry the burden of memory, but not always. Dina Wardi in *Memorial Candles: Children of the Holocaust* (London, Routledge, 1992) has pointed out in most survivor families one child is designated as a 'memorial candle' for the relatives who died in the Shoah and 'is given the burden of participating in his parents' emotional world to a much greater extent than any of his brothers or sisters' (p. 6), thus freeing the siblings from some of the trauma. Such children are often named after dead relatives and can feel that they have to live up to the lost relative's idealized memory. Anne Karpf recalls that Art Spiegelman, the American cartoonist of Maus, refers to the blurred photograph of his 'ghost brother', killed age five or six, before he was born, which hung in his parent's bedroom:

> The photo never threw tantrums or got in any kind of trouble . . . It was an ideal kid, and 'I' was a pain in the ass. I couldn't compete. They didn't talk about Richieu, but that photo was a kind of reproach. 'He'd' have become a doctor and married a wealthy Jewish girl . . . The creep . . . It's *spooky* having sibling rivalry with a snapshot. [Art Spiegleman, *Maus 11,* Harmondsworth, Penguin Books, 1992, p. 15]

Aaron Haas noticed that he was often being asked by those who'd left Nazi Europe in the late 1930s if they, too, fell under the rubric of survivor. He concluded that 'The question has a pleading quality, the questioner seeks grace . . . The question reflects the need to identify with those who suffered, and the disquieting belief that they themselves did not suffer enough.' Anne Karpf recalls that Robert Jay Lifton remarks that guilt moves in concentric circles from the dead themselves:

> The survivors feel guilty towards the dead; those who just missed going through the experience feel guilty towards the survivors; those who were even further away feel guilty towards the latter group.

But this should just make us more wary about how we speak about gradations of suffering and understand claims to membership of particular victim groups. Karpf is surely right that

> It would be dreadful if being a child of survivors became, in some perverse way, a desirable badge of victimhood. It seems difficult for us to maintain the distinctiveness of different historical experiences without ranking them in order of importance and grading their suffering, but my own view is that there were real similarities and real differences in the experiences of refugees and survivors and their children and they both need acknowledging. The Nazis

saw the Jews as a homogenous group, defined only by ethnicity; it behoves us to be able to examine our differences. [Anne Karpf, *The War After* (London, Minerva, 1997), p. 241]

Sharings

Anne Karpf shares her experience of taking her father to the Jewish Film Festival in London to see a documentary about pre-war Polish Jewish life. She recalls

> Its images of vanished communities filled me with regret and yearning. I was astonished at how like me those young, amused women looked: if the war hadn't happened, that's where and how I'd have been, and this fantasy of being on the inside, among similars, intrigued me. [Anne Karpf, *The War After* (London, Minerva, 1997), p. 139]

This is a feeling of identification that I know for myself, as if I am looking for signs I might almost be able to remember, a family name or town I could claim. But Anne Karpf's father was ready to share his reminiscences but she was aware that his nostalgia about pre-war Poland was terribly unsentimental. As she puts it

> though he fiercely wanted us to know about his past, at the same time there was a kind of detachment in the way he described pre-war Poland, and the same went for my mother. Bizarrely, I felt as if I were more sentimental about their past lives than they were: I was horribly aware that their lives had been bisected, but whereas they always seemed to accept the bisection and fully inhabit the second half, I was in some way always trying to recover the former half, for which I felt an enormous sense of loss. [Anne Karpf, *The War After* (London, Minerva, 1997), p. 139]

Admitting to these longings makes her feel a little embarrassed, as she put it, for it seems excessive and, given that she is British born, inappropriate. Only later did she discover how common such a sense of longing is among children of survivors and refugees, as if the children are somehow feeling the loss for their parents – loss that they refuse or are unable to feel for themselves. Returning to London from a trip to Poland, Anne showed her mother photos of all the homes in which she had lived. She poured over the photos with pleasure and interest, as if they were fascinating historical documents belonging to someone else's life. Then she put in a cassette of a song by Mordechai Gebirtig. Her mother had been a close friend with one of his daughters, Siwka, with whom she went to school. She sometimes heard the father humming a tune as he worked. Only later was he recognized as a fine composer of Yiddish music. She played her mother *Unser Shtetle Brennt* ('Our Town's on Fire), an evocative piece of music that my partner, Anna, also remembers her own mother singing to her when she was a child. The music had somehow penetrated where the pictures and words could not.

As Anne describes it

> my mother crumpled into a terrible shocked sadness and began to sob . . . I switched off the cassette-player immediately, and apologised again and again for upsetting her, but already she's begun to talk: 'When I think of all the people I lost – my brother, my father (and she named a long list), I don't know why I didn't hang myself. How could I survive, go on living after all that, and after losing Josef too?

Anne shares her own questioning, which followed later:

> I wonder why I did it. Why did I try and force her to reconnect with all that she'd lost? Sadism, or revenge for all those years of feeling impelled to look after her? A wish for her to take back some of the grief which I'd carried for her, and which now felt intolerably burdensome? Or some perverse desire to see her whole, inhabiting not only the triumphant but the sad parts of herself as well? Or all of these? Whatever the reason, the moment it had occurred and I glimpsed the sheer drop of her grief, its awe-inspiring dimensions, I regretted it deeply, but already she's recovered, saying 'Yet I get up and I'm happy to be here in this lovely flat, and to live.' I also reminded her, unnecessarily, of all she had to live for – her children, friends, music, and grandchildren. [Anne Karpf, *The War After* (London, Minerva, 1997), p. 311]

As adults we can still feel that there are stories that we need to hear and feelings we need to share without parents. Often we return in the hope that this time it might be different, but usually it is not. It takes time to realize that if we cannot hope for our parents to change, then we have to change ourselves, to do the emotional work for ourselves so that we can offer something different to our children, whilst honouring what our parents have been able to offer to us. As children of the second generation we do not want to cause them more pain than they have already suffered and often we instinctively protect them. But sometimes our lives are enmeshed with their histories and unspoken tragedies. Often we never hear what we think we need to hear for ourselves and we are left with gaps that cannot be crossed. We have to learn to live, as Moshe Halevi Spiro has it, quoted in Karpf, as part of a definition of a 'second generation syndrome' with 'transmitted absences, vacuums, denials, gaps, and intergenerational psychic holes' (p. 230). As we learn to name these experiences for ourselves and touch their reality, so we can begin to identify the 'differences' that we also feel, without the self-blame and self-accusation that can often accompany it. Rather than feel there is something 'wrong' with us, we begin to appreciate the particularities of our histories, and also hopefully ways of emotionally working with it to find greater freedom and self-acceptance.

Anger

A common theme in the literature on children of the Holocaust is their difficulties in expressing anger towards their parents. It can feel as if they are not entitled to their own anger and as if to express any anger towards their parents is a sign of ingratitude, given everything they have already been through. Often parents had to suppress their own rage during the Holocaust, for this could threaten their very lives and safety, so children can later experience their own normal aggressive instincts as over-whelming. It could be difficult to question parents who felt that they always had to be 'right' and in control of situations and who found it difficult to tolerate any kind of ambivalence. This could create too much anxiety for the parents to deal with. The parents had often learned to be active as an important adaptive defence mechanism in the camps, for when camp inmates couldn't go on working this would usually mean selection for the gas chambers or other forms of death. Often they did not want to hear what their children were going through, if it was sadness or depression, because this threatened to trigger their own unresolved feelings.

In refugee families the experiences were different. Certainly refugees and survivors shared both the pre-war experiences of discrimination and the threat and often actual experience of violence, as well as post-war experiences of discovering the death of parents and families. Both groups also experienced the trauma of relocation and loss of homeland. There was also a sense of rejection and a feeling of abandonment on the part of the countries people had grown up to love. I know from my own experience how these unresolved feelings can be 'passed on' and the ways you learn to suppress your own feelings because they never seem to matter as much, as your parents. Sometimes there is intolerance of emotions and of therapy generally, as if it was a sign of madness. Often you learn to put your emotions aside and to carry on regardless. This is often the unconscious message that is passed on. You learn to fear your own vulnerability, as you also learn to fear your anger. At some level you learn to think 'what is the point?' when you can do so little about it. It is better to put your emotions aside and 'look positively', on the bright side. There is no point looking back to a life that is gone or to dwell upon sufferings that you cannot transform.

If there is a question of how can you 'grieve' when there is so many who were killed, there is also a question of how you can express anger. What kind of anger could be appropriate to the enormity of the loss? Yael Danieli quotes a person who feels unable to express anger because it is bound to be overwhelming : 'My rage is so big it will consume everyone. Almost like a Holocaust.' ('The Impact of Holocaust Experience on Families of Survivors Living in the United States' in *The Nazi Concentration Camps,* Proceedings of the Fourth Yad Vashem International Historical Conference, Yad Vashem, 1984, p. 116). It is common for people to feel uneasy about releasing anger which has been suppressed for so long, but there is a particular intensity when you are dealing with the scale of Nazi atrocities. The rage can feel limitless, as if it would go on forever. But this can make it more important to create safe settings in which some of this anger can be explored. It becomes important to distinguish between the anger and rage you might be carrying for your parents and the anger and rage you feel for yourself.

During the events to mark the fiftieth anniversary of the release of prisoners from the camps, it was often asked, especially by Christian theologians 'is it not time to forgive, if not to forget?' Primo Levi made clear that it is not for the survivors to offer forgiveness for those who perished. The only ones who could do this have died. Often Jews feel that they want to see justice done and do not want to feel that time makes any difference to the need to pursue perpetrators of these crimes against humanity. This is equally true for the crimes committed in Bosnia. This is a matter of justice and not vengeance, though there is often an unspoken implication that Jews somehow believe in revenge – the Biblical notion of an eye for an eye whilst Christianity supposedly believes in forgiveness. Often it is said that, unless you can reach a point of forgiveness, you cannot move on in your own life. This is something Leo Baeck appreciated, fearing that people might feel stuck in their feelings for revenge, unable to move forward.[8] These are complex issues that link to traditions of Christian anti-Semitism and that find their ways into modern forms of philosophy and social theory that, in crucial respects, are unknowingly built upon secularized Protestant traditions, particularly in their disdain for the body and emotional life as sources of knowledge.

However uncomfortable it might make people feel, the second and third generation need to find ways of expressing the anger and rage they carry, lest otherwise it poison them. Very little of this has been expressed because it remains threatening and it is easy to feel that emotions are 'irrational' and 'unreasonable'. Strong emotions can feel at odds with a middle-class English education. But at another level children were often aware of the suppressed rage that their parents carried. Sometimes this rage would break through the surface and children would glimpse what their parents were silently carrying. This could be scary for children who might learn to fear emotions in general, feeling that they needed to be kept in tight control. It could be difficult to learn to trust others with your emotions, growing up in families in which you often learned that only family can be trusted – friends might turn out to betray you in the end.

But often in the families parents were so preocupied with themselves and with the need to make a living, that they expected their children to almost bring themselves up. Children learned not to provide their parents with extra burdens so they soon learn to keep their emotions and feelings to themselves. The parents had suffered enough and emotions came to be identified as further burdens for parents who were often emotionally inaccessible to their own children.

If parents refuse to express their own anger, it can make it more difficult for children to acknowledge the anger they carry for their parents too. Fearful of being overwhelmed, it can feel easier to deny the anger, but then it can be difficult to come to terms with what happened. You can feel trapped by the unreality of the 'six million' unable to get through to feeling for the individuals who were lost. This is an issue in Holocaust education but also for parents who feel a need to share their family histories with their children. Sometimes it can feel easier to put it off until the child is 'old enough to understand'. But unless we have done some of this difficult emotional work around anger, grief and loss, it is difficult to feel that the time is ever 'right', and it will be tempting to put it off again. But we need to be clear about our own stories, before we can feel ready to share with our children. We have to feel ready to do the emotional and intellectual work so that we can find some inner balance within ourselves, so that we are ready to listen to whatever feelings come up in our children.

Again this is part of a parenting relationship that might have a very different quality from what we have know with our parents. If we want to stay in connection with our children we will need to share this inheritance with them, whilst also recognizing the joys and enduring values of a Jewish spiritual tradition. But if we have been cut off from these traditions ourselves, we have to be careful not to create new Jewish identities through the Holocaust alone. This would create a victim identity that our children will often reject. We must recognize the values and traditions of the culture that was destroyed, for this was part of the evil that was done. Rather than turn away from these diaspora cultures to look towards Israel alone, we have to learn *how* to honour and value a past that was too readily shamed, not only in the eyes of the dominant Christian culture, but for Jews themselves. This possibly remains a particular responsibility for the second generation as they learn to also honour what their parents went through, while finding their own light to live in.

Notes

1. For an illuminating discussion of the relationship of the Holocaust to modernity, see Zygmunt Bauman, *Modernity and the Holocaust* (Cambridge, Polity Press, 1989). This is an issue I have also attempted to explore in the concluding chapter of *The Moral Limits of Modernity: Love, Inequality and Oppression* (London, Macmillan, 1991).
2. For some helpful reflections upon the nature of self-identity see, for instance, Anthony Giddens, *Modernity and Self-Identity* (Cambridge, Polity Press, 1991); Charles Taylor, *Sources of the Self* (Cambridge, CUP, 1989), and Lionel Trilling, *Sincerity and Authenticity* (Cambridge, Harvard University Press, 1978).
3. For some helpful reflections upon the difficult relationships between memory and mourning, see for instance, see Phyllis Grosskurth, *Melanie Klein* (London, Karnac Books, 1987); Alexander and Margarete Mitscherlich, *The Inability To Mourn* (London, Grove Press, 1975) and Shoshana Feldman and Dori Laub, *Testimony: Crisis of Witnessing in Literature, Psychoanalysis and History* (London, Routledge, 1992).
4. Anne Karpf has written movingly in *The War After* (London, Minerva, 1997) about her experience of growing up in post-war Britain as the child of survivors, as well as exploring the history of British attitudes towards the Jews. She also investigates the literature on the second generation and the psychological after-effects of the Holocaust.
5. For an understanding of Freud's thinking about mourning see 'Mourning and Melancholia' in *The Standard Edition of the Complete*

Psychological Works of Sigmund Freud, trans. James Strachey et al., 24 vols (London, Howarth Press, 1953 vol 14: 240–59).

6. Janine Chasseguet-Smirgel, as reported in a footnote in Anne Karpf, *The War After,* p. 326, recounts that 'supervisions . . . show that many analysts – both Jewish and non-Jewish for that matter – are unable to recognise material connected with the Shoah. For instance, for a Jewish patient, a train is seldom an excursion train' 'Time's White Hair We Ruffle,' *Reflections on the Hamburg Congress, International Review of Psycho-Analysis,* no. 14, 1987, p. 434).

7. Some of the issues relating to the ambivalence in relation to Jewish identities within modernity have been opened up by Zygmunt Bauman, *Modernity and Ambivalence* (Cambridge, Polity, 1993). For an exploration of the ways that a liberal moral culture could seek to avoid issues related to the Holocaust, see Tony Kushner, *The Holocaust and the Liberal Imagination* (Oxford, Basil Blackwell, 1994).

8. For a sense of the intellectual and cultural context in which Leo Baeck was writing, see Albert Friedlander, *Leo Baeck – Teacher of Theresienstadt* (New York, 1968). For a sense of his own writings see, *Judaism and Christianity: Essays by Leo Baeck* (New York, Atheneum, 1981).

8

Creating Identities

Loss

Sidney Hershberg was 14 and a half when the Nazis marched into his hometown of Tern, in the Polish corridor between Germany and East Prussia. His middle-class family was forced to flee, leaving behind all their possessions. 'We left our house and everything was taken by the Germans' (*Jewish Chronicle*, 5 December 1997, p. 7). Although he is not sure whether his family had gold – 'which Jewish family did not have some kind of gold and silver?' the London conference, held in early December 1997 to shed light on what happened to large amounts of gold seized by the Nazis, has sparked a lot of dark memories for him and many other survivors (*Jewish Chronicle*, 5 December 1997, p. 3). Dr Chaim Dasberg, a retired professor of psychiatry and a clinical advisor to Amcha – the Israeli centre for psychological support for Holocaust survivors said that 'The report of stolen money and gold brings up memories of their stolen houses, their stolen books, their stolen countries and their stolen childhood' (p. 3).

Opening the conference on Tuesday, 2 December, Robin Cook, British Foreign Secretary, told delegates.

> We must avoid the second tragedy of those who survived the Nazis being left to live out their days in poverty. The real victims of the Nazis were not the central banks. They were individuals – countless individuals, who died because of their religion, their race, their beliefs.
>
> And we must always remember that they were individuals – because the Nazis tried so hard to reduce them to numbers, to remove their humanity. [*Jewish Chronicle*, 5 December 1997, p. 1]

Lord Janner said that the conference had been 'a great international recognition of a moral debt, of justice so long delayed, and so long denied' (*Jewish Chronicle*, 5 December 1997, p. 1).

But this is not easy to do, for how do we remember them 'as individuals' and what makes it so difficult to do so? Jews were not seen as individuals and even the liberal moral culture in the West did not give their individualism the moral basis it needed to defend them. This is not simply an issue that divides an Enlightenment West from the different traditions that flourished in the East. For if we have to think differently about the situation of Jews, say, in Poland and in Holland, we face vital issues in these diverse situations. If Jews were given citizenship within France, Germany and Holland this was not a citizenship that protected them.[1] When French Jews gained emancipation in 1791, Count Stanislas Clermont-Tonnerre declared in his famous declaration to emancipate the Jews: 'We must refuse the Jews everything as a nation and give them everything as individuals; they must constitute neither a political group nor an order within the state; they must become citizens as individuals' (quoted in Judith Friedlander, 'Anti-Semitism in France, 1978–1992' in Lawrence D. Kritzman (ed.) Auschwitz and After: Race, Culture and 'the Jewish Question' in France, (London, Routledge, 1995), p. 64).

These haunting words remain through the generations, for 'as individuals' the Jews were not protected as citizens.[2] Rather this was a strategy that served to disempower them. They were to exist as 'free and equal' citizens and were to treat their Jewishness as a matter of individual belief alone. They were to assimilate as best they could within Western Europe, learning to treat other Jews as their 'co-religionists' while learning that their primary identities were to be as either Germans, French, Dutch and English. If there were anti-Semitic notions circulating within the culture these were deemed to be 'backward' emotions that would inevitably give way, with progress, to an Enlightenment reason. In Germany it made Jews feel that Hitler and Nazism had to be a temporary political phenomenon, which would disappear in a short time.

Those who escaped felt fortunate and they also felt grateful to countries like England that allowed them in after *Kristallnacht*. They knew how difficult it was to find safety and it was difficult to feel angry at the same time that so few were allowed in and then only after a public protest against restrictive government policies. They felt grateful that they had survived when so many were to perish so that after the war it was difficult for them to feel anger at the governments that had allowed them in. Rather, they were to idealize Britain in a way that made it harder for the second generation to connect to their own anger. This was not just a matter of expressing the anger they carried for their parents, but it allowed them to feel their own anger at the loss and displacement. Many Jews in the Second Generation were scared of their own emotions and suspicious of psychotherapies that could have possibly enabled them both to separate from their parents as well as connect to the sources of their own anger and loss. Often this was overshadowed, as the second generation were resolved that what their parents had gone through 'would never be forgotten'. But the danger of this is in unwittingly maintaining a victim position, rather than learning to move beyond it.

At one level people can feel this is my parents' history; it is not mine. But this can make it difficult for people to recognize how much of their parent's unresolved emotions are being *carried* by the next generation. It can also be the case that, after some time, the children do not want to hear and take in what their parents have gone through, although at another level they have long requested the conversation. For sometimes they do not know what to do with this information and feel uneasy about what responsibilities it leaves them with. A woman whose mother had been in Auschwitz was hoping to drop in to see her mother on a trip back from the north to finally talk through some of her history. As she arrived, her mother gave her a parcel in which she had written out some of her experiences for her daughter, saying that she was willing to talk it through whenever she was ready. Months later, the daughter still found it difficult to 'find the time'. At some level she feels uneasy about having a conversation that has been delayed for so long. It has been easier for her mother to talk to her daughter, her grandchild, than it has been to communicate directly with her. This was also true of Anna's mother who could tell me things, while Anna might be sitting there, that she could not tell her. She had sought to protect her daughter for so long from this knowledge that it was difficult to break the pattern.

But the second generation can also feel ambivalent about what responsibilities might flow from this knowledge. It can involve 'emotional work' to establish their own emotions towards this knowledge, not just their parents' feelings, which they might carry. We might feel angry at what our parents were obliged to go through and because of the sufferings they endured, but we might also feel angry for the losses we have suffered as a consequence in our own lives. Psychotherapies can help us discover the 'objects' for the anger we carry, but this can also involve transforming the familial frameworks of traditional therapies. We might need to come to terms with the 'gratitude' we are supposed to feel for finding a place of refuge, as if Jews live in England as a 'minority' that needs to constantly prove its value to the host community. It was the politics of assimilation that dominated the post-war period and that fostered a hope that at least the children of refugees and survivors could 'become' English. There was a sense of being a 'tolerated' minority that made it difficult for the second generation to feel that they really 'belonged' or that they were entitled to feel angry at the collusions of so many in the British establishment with the Nazi leaders.[3]

As time passes there is also a pressure to leave history behind and to 'forgive, if not forget'. Here there is an unresolved tension between Christian notions of 'forgiveness' and the appropriation of love through a refusal to acknowledge the central place of love in the Jewish writings and the designation of Judaism as more concerned with justice as an 'eye for an eye'.[4] So Jews can be reminded of their refusal to forgive, which is taken as a sign of their 'stubborn' resistance to leaving history behind. This tension is reinforced within a post-modern culture that tends to treat history as a limitation, refusing to acknowledge the opportunities available in the present. This fosters a distrust of continuity as having little value in itself. Many young Jewish people can feel that, if they do not believe in religion then Judaism might be part of their past but it has little meaning and significance for them in the present. They might feel some ident- ification with the culture and look for ways of passing on a secular tradition to their children, but find it difficult to do so. They do not bring up their children with any sense of the festivals and rituals, so that those children feel even more distant than their parents. This forsaking of traditions remains a strong temptation within a post-modern culture that is wary of collective identities. At some level it shares in the disdain of a rationalist modernity in the ways it refuses to acknowledge emotional and spiritual life. It becomes even more difficult to name what has been lost.

Naming

How do we learn to identify our own history? Whose sufferings do we feel for? Do we have to learn to identify with the sufferings of our own particular group to be able to feel for the sufferings of others too? Do we have to name our histories if we are to feel a fuller sense of identity in the present? Within a post-modern culture there has been a weakening of any sense of historical consciousness, as people often feel a radical break between the present and the past they might hear about.[5] They might learn about the past in history lessons, but find it difficult to *connect* this to the present. This might be true of African-Americans learning about slavery as it is for young Jews learning about the Holocaust. The idea that you can only know 'who you are if you know where you have come from' is in tension with a post-modern sensibility that focuses upon ways we create identities out of what is culturally available for us in the present. We might draw upon the past, but we should not allow ourselves to be limited by it.[6]

The ways people make connections with their past, and so with themselves, very much depends upon the cultural and social context. Within a culture of liberal individualism it can be difficult to connect to a shared history and culture. But events take place that can shock people into a sense of self-recognition, as has happened recently in Holland with the tales of wartime Germany's neighbours and victims profiteering from the crimes of the Nazis. The revelations of government functionaries in Holland queuing to bid for valuable plundered from the Dutch Jews in the 1940s has triggered a sense of shame, disgust, and embarrassment. The Amsterdam weekly magazine, *De Groene Amsterdam,* reported that up until the 1960s the Dutch Finance Ministry was still in possession of gold, silver, jewellery, and household valuables looted by the Nazis. The property was never reclaimed because the owners were murdered in the Nazi death camps. Rather than hand it over, the Finance Ministry organized an internal and clandestine auction among its employees.

'Who would give his wife a present of earrings taken from a Jewish woman gassed in Auschwitz?' asked the daily *De Volkskrant* newspaper. The answer seems plain. As Ian Traynor reported the story in the *Guardian:*

> The demand for a slice of the loot was so great that officials drew lots to determine who would take part in the sale. Whistle blowers, outraged at the goings-on in the finance ministry told De Groene Amsterdamer that some of the successful bidders were 'dancing for joy' in the office.
>
> 'The things were laid out and sold off as bargains, My colleagues let anyone see what they had brought,' said an unnamed retired finance ministry official. 'Of course, these people knew that what they were buying had come from the Jews. These people had no feelings.' [Guardian, 15 December 1997, p. 13]

As Ian Traynor reminds us, 'Every February, the Dutch mark the strikes and protests that accompanied the anti-Semitic pogroms of February 1941, celebrating the national self-image of anti-Nazi resistance' (p. 13). But the revelations have tarnished this self-image and raised questions about Dutch historical memory. Dutch Jewish leaders say that the auction was 'the tip of the iceberg' and that investigations are likely to show up details of Dutch banks dealing in Nazi gold, of trading in looted art, and of the bureaucracy created to frustrate Holocaust survivors' efforts to recover their belongings. The Nazis had taken over the Lippman-Rosenthal Bank, founded by Amsterdam Jews in 1859, which was to become the main depository for expropriated Jewish accounts, money, and valuables. The idea was that the Dutch Jews were more likely to place their valuables with what had been a well-known Jewish Bank. At least 13,000 deposits were made and the bank opened up a branch at the Westerbork transit camp, from where Dutch Jews were sent to the death camps. As Traynor reports 'from 1942 they had to surrender household valuables – gold, silver, platinum, coin collections and objects d'art – to the bank' (p. 13). They were given receipts and the deposits were meticulously entered in the ledgers – as the Liro archives, which had long been though lost and destroyed, have recently shown.

These revelations are forcing people to face their histories anew but they are also creating reverberations in Jewish communities who have to face how readily abandoned they were. They have even been used to sustaining images of the resistance and to hiding the levels of collaboration that have been revealed recently in different European countries. Many of these objects carried feelings and memories for families who had lost so much during the war. The Nazis had been careful to strip people of their possessions, for they knew this was a way to attack their identities and sense of self-worth. These objects are not simply sources of wealth but they are the carriers of memories and they can help people to a sense of their own personal histories. But Jews were to be denied their humanity, which is crucially tied to a sense of particularity. Jewish women, for instance, were not to be allowed their personal names, but they were to be uniformly named by the Nazis as 'Sarah'. They were to be interchangeable and so rendered 'less than human'.

Dutch Jews returning from the camps had been told by government officials that records of valuables confiscated during the war had been lost. But, in early December 1997, meticulous records detailing the names and addresses of owners, as well as subsequent buyers, were found in a former Ministry of Finance building. Christophe Rocour, aged 28, stumbled upon the archives while visiting a friend who was housesitting the vacant building. According to the *Utrechts Nieuwsblad* newspaper, as reported in the *Jewish Chronicle*

the Finance Ministry's first reaction to the discovery was: 'Of course those students should never have opened those (archive) drawers.'

Members of the Jewish community, though angry, were not greatly surprised at the ministry's negligence, 'It fits in nicely,' said Herman Loonstein, who deals with claims against Dutch banks, 'The government has done nothing whatsoever to trace survivors and their descendants in order to return stolen property. This is a typical, if horrific, example.' [*Jewish Chronicle,* 19 December 1997, p. 2]

Contempt

A Polish minister, Krysztof Sliwinski, whose portfolio includes relations with diaspora Jewry, specifically wanted to see a Beth Jacob School for Jewish girls in North London, on a recent visit to England in December 1997 because the first Beth Jacob school was founded in Krakow in 1917. Anna went to a similar school in New York when she arrived there from Germany with her parents after the war. They had survived the camps and had met and lived together for a short time in Regensburg where she was born. Mr Sliwinski, a former university lecturer, spoke about the importance of the recent renewal of the Jewish community in Poland.

> I remember there were really demonical forces that wanted to annihilate the Jews, and not just in the Holocaust.
>
> Many Poles say it is wonderful that our country is 98 per cent Polish, but it makes me feel like a limb has been amputated.
>
> There is now an enormous search to learn about the Jewish past. I don't pretend that anti-Semitism will disappear overnight, but it will become more marginal. [*Jewish Chronicle,* 5 December 1997, p. 3]

There is an analogy between the complex relationships of Poles and Jews and the historical relationship between Christians and Jews. In the Declaration of Repentance made by the Roman Catholic Bishops of France at Drancy, the detention camp outside Paris, on 30 September 1997, it was recognized that Jacques Maritain and others endeavoured to show Christians another way of perceiving the Jewish people. They remember that

> During the war theologians and exegetes in Lyon and Paris prophetically emphasised the Jewish roots of Christianity, highlighting that the root of Jesse blossomed in Israel, that the two Testaments were inseparable, that the Virgin, Christ and the Apostles were Jews, and that Christianity is linked to Judaism like a branch to the trunk which bore it. Why was so little attention paid to these words? [*Common Ground,* number 3, 1997, p. 4]

The tree of life was not only broken – it was to be dug up and destroyed so that possibly attention would never have to be given to rethinking the complex and tragic relationships between Judaism and Christianity.

The Declaration is an important step that other Churches have still to make. It begins with the recognition that

A major event in the history of the 20th century, the Nazi endeavour to destroy the Jewish people raises formidable questions that no human being can sweep aside. The Catholic Church knows that conscience is stirred by remembrance and that no society or individual can be at peace if their past has been repressed or wrongly represented. [*Common Ground,* number 3, 1999]

The Shoah is not an issue for Jews alone, but the post-war intellectual culture often refused to recognize the nature of the challenges it presented to modernity as a project of a secularized Christianity. For a long period, Christianity had the power to forget and to represent Jewish history, traditions and culture in the form that best suited itself. This is why the willingness of the French bishops to submit their own history 'to a critical reading, without hesitating to acknowledge the sins committed by its sons, and to ask forgiveness from God and from men' (p. 3) is so important.

The bishops acknowledge that they could have done more during the months following the defeat of 1940, when state anti-Semitism became rife, depriving French Jews of their rights and foreign Jews of their freedom. They failed to speak up when 'the impact of a public statement might have forestalled an irreparable catastrophe' (p. 3). As the Declaration acknowledges

Anti-Semitic legislation enacted by the French government deprived a French social grouping of their rights as citizens, ruining them and imposing upon them an inferior status within the nation. Decisions were taken to intern in camps foreign Jews who believed they could count on the right to asylum and on the hospitality of France. Therefore, there is no choice but to admit that the Bishops of France did not speak out, acquiesced through their silence in these fragrant violations of the rights of man and leaving an open field for the spiral of death. (p. 3)

But the statement goes further for it recognizes 'It is important to admit the primary role, if not direct, then indirect, played by the constantly repeated anti-Jewish stereotypes wrongly perpetuated among Christians in the historical process that led to the Holocaust' (p. 4). It goes on to acknowledge 'This soil nurtured the poisonous plant of contempt for Jews with its legacy of serious consequences which, until our century, have been difficult to remove. Wounds resulting from this contempt are still open and unhealed' (p. 4). If the will to remove them had been there actions could have been taken long ago, for these 'stereotypes' were not accidental but played a crucial part in the self-identity of dominant Christian traditions. But they willingly admit that the fact remains that, although courageous actions in defence of persons were not lacking, we must acknowledge that indifference largely prevailed and, in the face of persecution of Jews, especially the multi-faceted anti-Semitic laws passed by Vichy, silence was the rule and words in favour of the victims the exception.[7]

As Francois Mauriac wrote, 'a crime of this proportion redounds in no small part on all the witnesses who did not protest and on those who were responsible for their silence.'

The result was that the attempt to destroy the Jewish people, instead of being perceived as a central concern on the human and spiritual level, remained a secondary issue.

Dispensable

Many Jews still carry the feeling that they were to be abandoned by the West and that they were to remain 'a secondary issue' as regards the war effort too. However, there were many individuals who risked their lives to rescue Jews and their examples remain an important example of righteous behaviour in the midst of darkness. As the Oliners showed in their study *The Altruistic Personality,* these were often individuals who had somehow developed individual beliefs for themselves.[8] Often they were marginal figures in their own community who had learned an ethic through a close and loving parental relationship. It was not the professions who stood up to be counted when it really mattered – rather, they often betrayed their Jewish colleagues. Nor was it the established Churches who were able to give a lead to resistance. Again, it was left to individual voices to speak out. It is these silences that remain a crucial challenge to prevailing ethical theories. We still have to ask the crucial questions about the collusive relationships between power and ethics and about the different ways we should be learning to speak to our children about values and beliefs.

Ann Karpf asks her mother whether she would have liked them to have bombed the camp? Her response is clear:

Yes, we prayed for it, that they would bomb. We used to say, 'Where is the world? Where is the United States? Where is Russia? Where is Britain?' And sometimes we prayed that we should go to sleep and never wake up, because we were humiliated, we were beaten, we were tortured, we were starved, and we saw such terrible sights that it was unbearable. And I still dream of it: I dreamt the other night again, then I woke up from that bad dream, and then I fell asleep and dreamt the same – that they want to arrest me, than I ran away and I hid, and I was terrified that they're going to find me. [Anne Karpf, *The War After* (London: William Heinemann, 1996), p. 89]

Somehow she had to learnt to live with terrible memories. Sometimes they are suppressed and passed on to the second generation who can find it difficult to name the fears and uncertainties they carry. It can be difficult to live with knowing what your parents went through so it can feel easier not to know, whilst you also know. Natalia Karpf learnt what had happened to her father on 1 June 1942. She received a telegram that her father had been taken from the ghetto on a transport. The conversation Anne Karpf, seeking to know more, had with her mother was:

AK: Did you know where he went, what camp he was taken to?

NK: What camp? If somebody was taken from the ghetto, he wasn't going to a camp, only to the oven. I felt absolutely crushed, shattered. One day, before the ghetto had been established, they started gathering all the Jews of Turnoff in a big square, and shooting them. They didn't take us, but they shot 15,000 people in one day. It was a massacre. We heard the shooting all day long. Before that we had to go to the Gestapo headquarters to get a card with a stamp: those with a stamp didn't have to go to the square.

AK: On what basis did they give you a stamp?

NK: Who knows? Whether their nose was nice, or they wore spectacles, or didn't wear spectacles, or had a beard – who knows? We were so terrified all the time: whenever I heard the sound of bootsteps behind me and 'Halt', I always thought that I feel a bullet through my head. I had a stamp, so I didn't have to go to the square, but my sister didn't have one, so I was in hysterics over what to do with her. I had some friends who had a stamp but were working in a clothing factory, and one said that she'd hide Helunia there, and she took her and hid her there for a few days. [Anne Karpf, *The War After* (London: William Heinemann, 1996), pp. 73–4]

The terror of not knowing what the criteria for selection might be, or whether there were any, leaves its own mark. Who would be chosen to live and who would be condemned to die? How could people sustain trust with each other in these circumstances? Yet it was often bonding with others that helped them survive. Natalia Karpf shares her own experience of going through a selection process at Plaszow.

On 14 May 1944 suddenly an Appel again – everyone on this big square. We had to stand there for six or seven hours. They put on the loudspeakers lullabies and songs of children singing 'Mummy', and we heard them taking, on open lorries, all the children, away from their mothers and from the camp – we knew it would be to a gas chamber somewhere. Wojtuc, who was then ten, was taken from Jelinek. We heard the screams of the children, and we had to kneel down and not look up. Can you imagine? Jelinek was in a terrible state, we were all, yet still in August she jumped into a trench. [Anne Karpf, *The War After* (London: William Heinemann, 1996), p. 84]

She goes on to talk of another occasion when there was a Selektion

and we had to undress and file naked past all these Gestapo men and outside, and they decided what to do with us : those who were thin were taken somewhere, those who had glasses were sent somewhere else. There were Selektions every few months, when we'd file past them and they'd choose who will live and who will die – they'd say 'Diese, diese, diese.' ('This one, this one, this one.') Cesia was very thin and I was always frightened that something might happen to her. And when I heard 'diese' behind me and Helunia was behind me. I couldn't look: but it was always someone behind her who'd been chosen. It was pure chance than the five of us survived the Selektions.

Many people became unbearable to be with – they were fighting for their survival, so they didn't care for other human beings. The Jewish kapos were humiliating us: Jelinek was always late for Appel – every morning we had to stand there and they counted us – and she was hit, beaten terribly.

The others used to say we'll never survive this, and I was always the optimist. I said, 'Don't talk like this – you will see we will survive, nothing will happen to us.' Sometimes I didn't believe it myself, but I thought, 'Why should I add to it? I'll give them hope.' I only wished I would go to sleep and not wake up any more – that's what I wished.

On Yom Kippur in 1944 in Plaszow I fasted. The others in the barracks laughed at me because they said, 'You fast the whole year here, how can you fast?' But I didn't eat anything that day. [Anne Karpf, *The War After* (London: William Heinemann, 1996), pp. 84–5)]

As the survivors and refugees retire and find they have more time on their hands, some of the memories return to haunt them. Some parents still want to keep these memories to themselves. Sometimes they have been invoked, if not spoken to invalidate the experience of their own children. 'You think you are sad, what do you know of sadness?' 'You think you are depressed, what can you know of depression?' 'If you are scared, I'll tell you things that will really make you scared.' So it is that many children of survivors learn that they are not entitled to their own feelings, so they learn to swallow them and keep them hidden. They learn not to acknowledge them, even to themselves. Sometimes the suppression of sensitivity shows itself on the surface of the skin, as Ann Karpf shares in relation to the skin as a boundary that she picked away at, to allow some of the poison that she was carrying to be released. In my own history,

I used to have a swelling of the skin surface that used to mean that my whole head would swell up. I could not look myself in the mirror without feeling a sense of revulsion because my features had become almost monstrous. I could not recognize myself. Sometimes I had to take time off school and wait for the swellings to subside.

But we were not really told what had happened before and during the war. There were hints that my mother's father had not 'got away in time'. We knew that he had gone East and that he had probably died in a camp near Drohobitch. But we did not know for certain so that we lived with the shadows. As I grew up I knew only vaguely that my father's family had been destroyed in Warsaw but I did not get to know any of the details until I was well into my adult years. As children we learnt not to ask questions, but this meant we did our best to make sense of what we knew. We learnt to compartmentalize our lives so that we could somehow be 'like everyone else' and, as I have said, for years I believed a myth that there was nothing unusual in the childhood we lived. There was a strong emphasis upon 'normality' and we learnt to deal with our emotions on our own. It was difficult to name what had been passed on to us, for it was often difficult to separate emotionally from parents who we wanted to protect because 'they had suffered enough'.

At some level we learned as children to live without a history of our own. We hoped that the history we learned at school might be able to fill some of the gaps or at least provide us with an alternative 'English' history that we might be able to identify with. We were determined to make this history a history of our own, because at some level we were also ashamed of the histories that our parents carried, though we could rarely admit this to ourselves. They wanted us to grow up to 'become' English 'like everyone else'. We learned to look towards the future and attempted to create these new identities for ourselves. We imagined a different past for ourselves, partly built out of what we had learned at school. It was only later that we positioned ourselves differently in relation to this history, that we learned painful truths of how the Crusades, for instance, involved the massacres of Jews in the Rhinelands. These revelations made us feel uncomfortable, but often we did not really know what to do with them. They become 'secondary'.

For years we learnt to create identities as if the Shoah had not really happened. We knew that something dreadful had taken place and we knew about 'six million' Jews who had perished. But at another level we did not know, or we could not 'take in', what had happened. We knew the images, which had become almost too familiar to us, so that they could not really be seen. We would look but often we could not see. We would hear what had happened and we might even have begun to collect whatever books and articles we might find, but often we did not read them. Often it was only much later, in our twenties and thirties, when we could begin to name some of our emotions, but then it could be difficult to name the anger, for coming from a refugee family we were always told that we had to feel grateful. It was also much later that I begun to realize just how few Jews were given permits and were able to escape. I slowly began to recognize what possibly should have been obvious, but somehow evaded me, that I was the child of a refugee family. I had been marked by the fears they carried, but it was difficult to feel entitled to think of them as 'survivors' too and ourselves, in some sense, as children of survivors.

This could have made me a little easier on myself and a little more forgiving of how different I often seemed to feel from others I knew. It was as if there had to be something 'wrong' with me, if I felt quite differently from other men that I knew. It was still easy to feel that I needed to judge myself through 'their' standards because if was 'others' who knew what it was 'to be English'. I had for so long had to learn to accommodate to what was expected of me that it was a long process of emotional work to begin to listen and respect my own feelings, beliefs and desires. If I felt strange or different, then I also had a different history and experience to come to terms with. I began to want to know more about the family history, but it was not always easy to get to know for I had to accept that my mother also did not know much about my father's family. It was difficult to accept that this history was part of what had been destroyed. But if we were to create new Jewish identities for ourselves, then this meant learning *how* to come to terms with such painful histories. Rafael Scharf recognized the issue himself in trying to share the history of Polish Jewry:

> The greatest difficulty as I see it, is how to present the boundless horror of those events which have no analogy in history and at the same time not to undermine the belief in the sense of creation, in human values, in justice. (*The Jewish Quarterly,* Autumn 1997, David Flusfeder talks to Rafael Scharf, p. 44.)

Notes

1. For some helpful discussion of the ways that liberal conceptions of citizenship failed to protect Jewish difference and made Jewish

communities vulnerable when rights were withdrawn by the state, see J.-P. Sartre, *Anti-Semite and Jew* (New York, Schocken Books, 1960); Avraham Barkai, *From Boycott to Annihilation* (Hanover and London, University Press of New England, 1989) and Carrie Supple *From Prejudice To Genocide: Learning About The Holocaust* (London, Trentham Books, 1992).

2. For an important discussion of emancipation within France see A. Hertzberg, *The French Enlightenment and the Jews* (New York, Columbia University Press, 1990) and for an insightful collection on the ways the Holocaust has been treated in France, Lawrence D. Kritzman (ed.) *Auschwitz and After: Race, Culture and 'the Jewish Question' in France* (London, Routledge, 1995).

3. [For some helpful discussion of the way that British society related to anti-Semitism and the Holocaust, see for instance David Feldman, *Englishmen And Jews: Social Relations and Political Culture, 1840–1914* (New Haven, Yale University Press, 1994); Richard Bolchover, *British Jewry And The Holocaust* (Cambridge, Cambridge University Press, 1993) and Tony Kushner, *The Persistence Of Prejudice: Anti-Semitism in British Society during the Second World War* (Manchester, Manchester University Press, 1989).]

4. I have explored issues in relation to different conceptions of love and power within Christian and Jewish traditions in *The Moral Limits Of Modernity: Love, Inequality and Oppression* (London, Macmillan's 1991). See also the illuminating discussions that touch on these themes in Emmanuel Levinas, *Difficult Freedom: Essays on Judaism* (London, The Athlone Press 1990) and *Outside the Subject* (London, The Athlone Press, 1993).

5. For a helpful discussion of some of the issues at stake in thinking postmodernism, see Zygmunt Bauman, *Modernity and Ambivalence* (Cambridge, Polity, 1993) and *Intimations of Postmodernity* (London, Routledge, 1992). See also Ulrich Beck, Anthony Giddens and Scott Lash (eds) *Reflexive Modernisation* (Cambridge, Polity, 1994).

6. For some illuminating discussion of how issues of identity, history and culture have been raised within an African American context, see, for instance, Cornell West, *Keeping Faith* (New York and London, Routledge, 1993) and bell hooks, *Talking Back: Thinking Feminist, Thinking Black* (Boston, South End Press, 1989) and *Sisters of the Yam: Black women and Self-Recovery* (London, Turnaround, 1993) and Audre Lorde, *Sister Outsider* (Freedom CA , Crossing Press, 1994).

7. A discussion of the role of Vichy in the 'Final Solution' is given in Serge Klarsfeld Vichy-Auschwitz, vol 1 and 2 (Paris, Fayard, 1983, 1985); Perre Birnbaum, *Anti-Semitism in France: A Political History from Leon Blum to the Present,* trans. Miriam Kochan (Oxford, Basil Blackwell, 1992); Michael R. Marrus and Robert O. Paxton, *Vichy France and the Jews* (New York, Basic Books, 1981) and Alain Finkielkraut, *Remembering in Vain: The Klaus Barbie Trial and Crimes Against Humanity* (New York, Columbia University Press, 1992).

8. The work completed by the Oliners draws upon interviews with rescuers in a number of different countries. See S. Oliner and P. Oliner, *The Altruistic Personality*: Rescuers of Jews in Nazi Europe (New York, Free Press, 1988). See also the illuminating study be Nechama Tec, *When the Light Pierced the Darkness: Christian Rescue of Jews in Nazi Occupied Poland* (New York, OUP, 1986).

9

Burdened by Memory

Poetry

Rafael Scharf acknowledges the commandment in the 'Shema', the key text of the Jewish liturgy, to teach the next generation, ceaselessly, the essence of Judaism. As David Flusfeder recognizes

> It's a necessarily injured kind of Judaism that Scharf is teaching, possibly the hardest and most noble type to maintain and the hardest to pass down. It's secular and agnostic, respecting the religious texts . . . but also respecting the canons of art and literature, from the modern era as well as the past. And it is dominated – but importantly, not limited – by the Shoah. (Scharf does not like the word 'holocaust': it means 'burnt offering'; to whom was the offering made?) [*The Jewish Quarterly*, Autumn, 1997, p. 41]

But he is very aware of the difficulties of living with this heritage in the second generation and the tensions that it creates for children who are growing up with an aspiration to be 'normal', to 'become English' and to be 'like everyone else'. We were to grow up in the shadows of the Shoah, to live as if, in some sense, it had not really happened at all. We knew that we did not have aunts and uncles and a family that we could call upon, but we learned not to make too much of this. It was important for our parents that we could live a life as normal as possible and that we enjoyed childhoods in which there was little missing. As my father died when I was just five, there was an added pressure upon my mother to somehow prove that we had not suffered unduly.

What does it mean to live as if you have a 'normal life' in circumstances that are far from normal? Is this a possible aspiration and would not the children eventually experience a deep sense of unreality in their own lives, for so much was being denied? Rafael Scharf puts this issue well when he asks :

How does one adjust to what, in ordinary life, passes for 'normality'? How does this awareness (of cataclysm, of loss of family) shape one's Weltan-schauung, one's perception of history, of religion, of morality, of man? The generation of Jews of the post-Holocaust era, the 'survivors' in the broadest sense, are a people apart. Burdened by memory, walking-wounded in eternal mourning. I do not think that an outsider can understand this condition. [*The Jewish Quarterly*, Autumn 1997]

Somehow this is a welcome description because it helps to name an inner experience that so often remains unnamed. It does not have to consolidate an image of being 'victims' but it can help us grasp some of the fears and uncertainties that we are constantly dealing with. This is a realization that can come slowly because if you grow up in the midst of the Jewish community, as we did in North London, you can be protected from an understanding that it was only a remnant that has survived, that Hitler came very close to completing the destruction of European Jewry. My family was lucky enough to escape, but they could never really explain to themselves why they had survived when so many had perished. This question remained at the edge of family life, though it was never put into words. But it remained a constant haunting presence.[1] After Anna Freud's initial work with child survivors came a prolonged silence until a two-day 'Survivor Syndrome Workshop' organized by the Group-analytic Society in London in September 1979. There was also the individual psychoanalytic work being done by Dinora Pines reported in 'The Impact of the Holocaust on the Second Generation' in Dinora Pines *A Woman's Unconscious Use of her Body* (London, Virago, 1993). Since the late 1980s there have been second generation groups as well as specialist psychotherapy services (Link, Shavalta, The Raphael Centre).

This can give a particular intensity to a question about what might make our lives 'meaningful', for often, as children, we could feel a pressure not only to redeem our own lives but also to 'make good' to redeem the lives of our parents too. Our parents could feel that they had survived to bring us into the world, and as children we could feel that we owed them a special debt of redemption. Sometimes this was framed universally for this could feel easier and, for a generation that came to maturity in the 1960s, this could also account for the intensity of political involvements in the early 1970s in the student movements. Unable to come to terms with the burdens of memory attached to our own Jewish-ness, many of us sought a revolutionary transformation that would redeem the whole community and so realize a prophetic vision of equality and justice. Although we had often been deeply identified with Zionism in our youth, often inspired by visits to Israel, it was difficult to maintain this vision as we became more aware of the rights of Palestinians and the realities of Israeli occupation.

Scharf celebrates his Krakow Hebrew schoolteacher, Benzion Rapp-aport, who was an inspirational teacher of ethics as much as religion. He inculcated 'the spirit of free-ranging, open-minded enquiry' and Rafael Scharf still remembers a lesson he taught him that went deep and which he still lives by:

> He took me aside and he told me I have never forgotten. 'Dear boy,' he said . . . 'The most important thing is the question man has to put to himself when he raises his eyes to heaven. *Ma chovato b'olamo* – what is my duty in this world? Every morning, before your begin your day, ask yourself this question – but seriously, not just casually. Every day afresh – and think about it a minute. Do not try to answer it – there is no short answer to it, it will not come to you quickly, maybe it will never come to you – it matters not. The thing is to realise that the question is important, that you have a duty to perform and have to search for it. [*The Jewish Quarterly,* Autumn 1997, p. 44]

This is a wonderful reminder that what matters is not so much the answer but taking time every day with the question. You have to give attention to the question without expecting that an answer will necessarily come and you have to be ready to accept that an answer might never come. This is a moral lesson that we can take to heart and it carries an added weight in the light of the Shoah, for we might find ourselves constantly asking questions that seem to have no answers. Sometimes it has taken consider-able time before we have been able to formulate helpful questions. In some way it also links to Joseph Brodsky's notion in his Nobel Prize acceptance speech, quoted by Scharf, that 'It is more difficult to break a man who reads poetry than one who does not' [Rafael Scharf, in *Poland, What Have I to do with Thee?* (Krakow, Foundation Judaica, 1996, p. 261]

He thinks of Max Boruchwowitz – Michal Borwicz – who describes how fragments of poetry were a 'kind of life-belt' in the camps. He was thinking of a 'selection' at the Janowski camp when his comrade, on the point of collapse

> begged his with his eyes for a word of solace, and how Borwicz then spoke aloud a couple of lines of poetry (some banal verses of his own, he says) and how these words, somehow, renewed his friend's failing strength and will to live. [Rafael Scharf, 'Let us talk;, in *Poland, What Have I to do with Thee?* (Krakow, Foundation Judaica, 1996), p. 262]

Indifference

Within Poland the Jews lived a largely separate existence and, as Scharf has it

> the culture which existed cheek by jowl, nay, right in the middle of the Polish community, remained totally unknown and uninteresting to the Poles, indeed they would have been staggered to be told that something was taking place her which deserved to be called culture. [Rafael Scharf, 'Let us talk, in *Poland, What Have I to do with Thee?* (Krakow, Foundation Judaica, 1996), p. 256]

There was a process of osmosis at the boundaries between the two communities, and it comprised the Jewish professional class and intellectuals who were a part of the Jewish community that identified with Polish national aspirations to a degree only possible under the regime of Pilsudski.[2] Janusz Korczak, the famous author and educator who ran a pioneering orphanage in Warsaw, was an example of someone who grew up feeling Polish to the core. He refused to wear the star of David because he felt that it did not represent his identification with Poland. He was attached to the Polish soil, history, literature and language. As Scharf has it

> In this he was typical of a segment of Jewish society in love with the idea of Poland. It was only by a gradual and painful process, in the cooling of the moral climate, that he was forced to recognise that his case was one of love unrequited, and no matter how pure and worthy his devotion he would stay condemned by the sheer fact of his origin. The unhealed wound of this rejection never ceased to plague him. [*The Jewish Quarterly,* Autumn 1997]

As anti-Semitism intensified, the process of assimilation became increasingly difficult and unrewarding, and this, as Scharf reminds us, 'it so happens, was in keeping with the instinctive stance of the overwhelming majority of the Jewish community. That majority was separated from the Polish community and all the more effectively as both sides favoured separation' (p. 257). There were professional contacts but very few social contacts.

The experience of a shared community in Poland was very different from Western Europe where Jews had often been able to assimilate and assume equal legal and political rights. There was a vision of liberal equality with which many Jews had learned to identify and they felt protected by it. But, as I have argued, this vision of liberal citizenship offered what was to turn out to be a false sense of security and sense of 'belonging'. Once the state chose to withdraw these rights, Jews were left bereft of an adequate sense of human dignity, for within the liberal state dignity came with rights. Individuals learned to think of themselves as the bearer of rights and they were wary of collective identities and looked down upon countries like Poland that failed to guarantee the same form of individual rights. As I have argued, Catholicism became the bearer of a precarious national identity, so that it was easy for Jews to feel excluded from the national community.

Scharf shows that other factors were also at work that help to explain why the greater part of the Polish community was insensitive to the fate of the Jews. Explaining the lack of social contacts he argues :

> The reasons for this were many, but the main one was that the Poles did not consider the Jews to be their equals as human beings. They looked down on us from a position of natural superiority. Regardless of their social positions, Poles, as a rule, considered themselves to be better and superior to Jews, any Pole to any Jew; superior, as it were, by definition. This lack of feeling of any common bond, the result of existing conditions, comes closest to explaining . . . that (though) there must have been vast numbers of good, ordinary people who were deeply shocked by the monstrous spectacle enacted in front of their eyes and who had genuine compassion for its victims, it is an undeniable fact that the majority of the Poles remained indifferent. [Rafael Scharf, *Poland, What Have I to do with Thee?* (Krakow, Foundation Judaica, 1996), p. 257]

As Scharf goes on to acknowledge, 'The Jews are bitterly resentful, but no one would claim that they were expecting it to be different – and that alone provides a tragic commentary' (p. 257) This anger is expressed not only against the Poles but against the world in which such things were possible and tolerated. He frames a question that is still very much with us:

> if, in our weakness or understandable concern for our own lives and the lives of those close to us, we are unable to behave morally and measure up to those high principles which we know from religion and philosophy and which we approve in theory, do we in such a situation consider our behaviour blameless and justified by rational requirements; or rather, are we left with a sense of shame that we did not live up to the call of conscience, shame increased by the knowledge that someone else – true, not many, but somebody, somewhere – did live up to it? I am putting these thoughts for consideration to those who sleep peacefully since, as they say, 'nothing could be done'. [Rafael Scharf, in *Poland, What Have I to do with Thee?* (Krakow, Foundation Judaica, 1996), p. 258]

These questions still haunt us, although for Jews they haunt us in different ways. We have our own questions about resistance and whether people resisted enough but we have also had to learn to respect different forms of resistance so that we do not slip into valuing military resistance alone. We each have to come to terms with our histories in our own ways and the moral issues they bring up for us. For years Jews expected little from the Poles except the admission that they had been, in some way, at fault. As Scharf recalls 'For many years we listened, waited for a sign – but we heard now voices. In the end, I had thought we would be straining our ears in vain. But now, at last – we have the voice of Blonski'[3] But the Church has remained largely silent and it has yet to feel the inner need and courage to carry out a self-examination like that of the French bishops. As Scharf has it:

> it will see with horror and contrition what role its immemorial and relentless anti-Judaism played in the extermination of the Jews – *in capite* and *in membris*. The record of the Polish Church with regard to the Jews is disgraceful – the sowing of hate does not yield a harvest of mercy. [p. 252]

Scharf also wanted to turn his back on Poland and forget his past but, as he says, the

> vaccine, as it were, did not take. I realised that were I, in some way, to shed my Polishness, be stripped of it – I would be damaged, impoverished, incomplete. Moreover, when I am thinking of those times, as I often do, the idea occurs to me – when it was so bad, why was it so good? [Rafael Scharf, 'As in a dream', in *Poland, What Have I to do with Thee?* (Krakow, Foundation Judaica, 1996), p. 264]

This can serve as a striking reminder for a second generation that was often brought up to feel that there was nothing but anti-Semitism to be followed by destruction. This was why it was so important for Anna and I to make our own trip to Poland and to explore these lost connections for ourselves. It was easy to feel that if Poland had few remaining connections for our parents, what it could mean for us as children who were born in different lands? Unlike Anna, I did not grow up hearing any Polish, though I might have had some idea that was where my grand-mother had come from. I knew that my father's family came from Warsaw and, before that, from Suwalki, but little more.

Roots

I met a friend whom I had not seen for a while at a neighbour's house. She was in her late forties and she had grown up in England, although her family had originally come from Poland. She had taken a number of steps towards her Jewishness, which had not meant much to her even ten years earlier. Somehow it had become important to her and she had become interested in knowing more about where her family had come from. As she described it, this had become the next step for her and she was interested in visiting Poland herself. This was not simply a nostalgic search for roots, but seemed to have to do with being able to heal herself in the present. It seemed to be part of a process of bringing some of the parts together. It did not mean that if she somehow recovered her roots, this would in some way allow her to know who she is. But this searching had become part of her growth and development, part of becoming, in Nietzsche's terms, who she is.

Postmodern discussions have helped to create their own scepticism about roots, as if it meant that we had to be 'rooted' in a single place, which would somehow give meaning and value to our lives. They question the promise of a more 'authentic' experience that is often tied up with these searches for roots, as if we could eventually come to know ourselves as 'authentic selves'. But if we are to welcome the fragmentation of postmodern identities, and if we are to be helped to recognize diaspora identities in which we learn to live between different places, learning to draw strength and sustenance from different sources, we should not simplify the difficulties attached to forming and sustaining hybrid identities.[4] If we have been brought up as post-Holocaust Jews to renounce our histories and to learn to look forward in an identification with Israel, rather than backward, where we often experience a black hole, a vortex that leads nowhere, we can often feel trapped in the present. We might be haunted by a sense of 'unreality' in the present, as if people can 'see through' us, as we learn to create adaptive identities in each new situation we meet.

Often Jews live in complex diasporas with complex histories and connections to different histories and cultures. It can be important to honour these connections, but it can be a slow process as people learn to acknowledge *how* they carry these different inheritances. Sometimes there are painful clashes, as parents have sought to make decisions for themselves that do not work for their children. Often this has to do with different ways of registering loss, but often this is obscured as post-modern identities often refuse to honour the past in their insistence on creating identities out of what is culturally available in the present. They find it difficult to retain a sense of 'keeping faith' with the past so that the past is remembered in ways that do justice to it. Often we have to find guides who can help us recover the complexity of memories that would otherwise be lost in a romanticization of the past. What needs to be recovered is the diversity of communities, secular and religious, cultural and political, that thrived in pre-war Poland. There were different visions of a shared conviction, as Scharf puts it

> that – irrespective of the poor living conditions and the daily struggles – man must aspire to things above the mundane, strive for a realisation of some high ideal, however defined. There was a deeply ingrained perception that decent behaviour towards fellow human beings, religious practice, the observance of ethical norms, respect for the scholar, pursuit of learning would speed the Messiah on his way and would initiate an era of universal justice. [Rafael Scharf, *Poland, What Have I to do with Thee?* (Krakow, Foundation Judaica, 1996), p. 265]

Rafael Scharf is concerned to cherish and cultivate the memory of Polish Jews within the modern world that has been characterized by fratricidal wars in the former Yugoslavia, Ireland, Russia and South Africa. In his opening speech at the inauguration of the Centre of Jewish Culture in Krakow, 24 November 1993, 'we will be able to point out that here, for centuries, despite everything, there existed a mode of co-existence, of a common life, of a symbiosis of two cultures resulting in mutual enrich-ment' (p. 266). If we have learnt to see the worst of what happened, we also have to learn to recognize the best if we are to reach a point, in Scharf's words, 'at which old wounds start to heal and a new generation grows up free from bigotry and prejudice'. He quotes a saying in Yiddish expressing a pious wish: *Fun dein mojl ins Gotts oyren* – let this go from your mouth to God's ear.

As he returned to Krakow after 'years stormy and turbulent', as Scharf puts it

> to cast an eye over the landscape of my youth and my childhood, where every stone is laden with sweet memories, to walk through the streets where our fates intermingled, where the street of Corpus Christi crossed with the Street of Rabbi Meisels, and the Street of Saint Sebastian with that of Berek Joselewicz . . . This was a community whose tone was set by Dr Osias Thin, the preacher in the liberal synagogue and a member of Parliament, Dr Ignacy Schwarzbart, a Zionist leader . . . Dr Chaim Hilfstein after whom the Hebrew

School was named; teachers of that school – Scherer, Haber, Mifelew, Rapaport, Katz, Szmulewicz, Feldhorn, Stendig, Waldman, Metalman, Mrs Goldswasser – many others, each of them deserving an epitaph of their own . . . the orthodox Rabbi Kornitzer, the assimilated chairman of the 'Kahal' Dr Landau : Wilhelm Berkhammer, Moses Kanfer . . . [Rafael Scharf, 'As in a dream', in *Poland, What Have I to do with Thee?* (Krakow, Foundation Judaica, 1996), p. 265]

and the list goes on.

As Scharf says

This sounds like a grey list of tenants, but for me it is anything but grey – every single name evokes, with poignant clarity, a distinctive face, movements, gestures, expressions, as if it were yesterday. I think of them with unfailing affection. I could find my way to their dwellings with my eyes shut, touching to be sure, the cavity on the side of the door where there used to be the 'mezuza'.

That human landscape is etched in my heart, my memory. I cannot forget for a single moment the majority of them, family, friends, acquaintances – none of them was a stranger to me – were hounded to death in the ghettos, in the labour camps, the death-factories, the gas chambers. We have got used to talking about this, using words derived from ordinary, everyday discourse, but nobody is able to take in the real meaning of that loss. [Rafael Scharf, 'As in a dream', in *Poland, What Have I to do with Thee?* (Krakow, Foundation Judaica, 1996), pp. 264–5]

How do we learn, as second generation, to talk about these happenings in a way that still has meaning for our children? This is something that we cannot do until we have struggled to make the loss meaningful for ourselves. This remains our task as we learn from our parents. But surely it becomes easier as we also learn to treasure the life that was lived there, so that we have more sense of what was destroyed. We have to recognize the diversity of values that were lived within these complex communities so that we do not begin to simplify the historical realities. A more pluralistic vision of the Jewish communities in Poland allows for a more textured grasp of Jewish–Polish relations. There were different ways of living out Jewish identities and antagonisms that had to be worked out between religious, ethnic, cultural, and political identities. There was a diversity that has often been difficult to honour within Western liberal societies, which have defined Jewishness in religious terms alone, as if it were a matter of religious belief so that if you did not share a belief, there could be no basis to your Jewishness. Sadly this creates its own forms of renunciation, erasure and disorientation.

As nation states begin to redefine themselves and more space is created for diverse identities that no longer feel the same pressure to assimilate into the dominant, hegemonic identity, so people can feel easier redefining their identities. As young Afro-Caribbeans and Asians have found, growing up in the New Britain of the 1990s, they can form their own hybrid identities, their own ways of 'being British'. There is a sense of entitlement that their parents might not have known – their parent's feeling that if they wanted to be 'accepted' then they had to be ready to separate from aspects of their cultures that would mark their differences. Young Jews have also been part of a process of reworking ethnic identification, learning to come to terms with being English and being Jewish. They no longer feel the same pressure to assimilate into the dominant Christian culture and can sometimes feel easier with themselves as Jews. But this is part of a process in which, as a 'third generation', many have to come to terms with their parents' histories and experiences. They face different realities and the war feels more distant from them, but they can also recognize the weakness of constructing Jewish identities in relation to the Holocaust alone. This produces its own forms of fear and resistance.[5]

I have tried to share some of my own process of exploration in relation to Jewish identity and belonging, as well as a particular journey to Poland that I made with Anna. This was a journey into the past but it also helped to redefine the present. But, crucially, it was part of a process that we had to go through for ourselves. We could support each other through it, but it was a path that we also had to be individually ready to take ourselves. It was a difficult journey and many fears began to surface as we prepared for it. If it was also a search for roots, it was done in recognition that many of us have complex roots that link us to different spaces and that many of the Jewish roots had been destroyed. We would be forced to search out cemeteries, the places of the dead, for signs of the living. I was also able to stand in front of a building that seemed to carry memories of its own. It is difficult to know how it helped, but it seemed to make a difference to both of us. When we returned we talked to our children about what we had experienced, knowing that they would make sense of it in their own way. But we also wanted to talk to them in ways that no one spoke to us as children. Of course we live in different times and different relations have become possible.

From the beginning it was the questions that were asked by Daniel and Lily about their own pasts and about their own spiritual beliefs that brought us back to our own questions. I know that this challenged me to ask questions about my own Jewishness. These questions were gendered from the beginning, because there is a privilege and recognition that

Judaism has traditionally given to boys but has denied to girls. This left me with easier feelings and less anger to deal with, but it also left us with a determination that our children should not suffer a similar discrimination and that the traditions needed to be reworked in more egalitarian and liberal directions. We could only pass on traditions that we could genuinely feel for, for otherwise we would be false to our own experience and this is something that children are very attuned to picking up for themselves. Often they learn by example and they reject, quite rightly, the notion that they should do what we say as parents, not what we do.

Judaism has been a tradition that has been constantly reinvented, whilst staying faithful to its core beliefs in justice, truth, and righteousness.[6] This does not mean that it is relative to existing cultures for it remains in a critical relationship with prevailing consumerist and materialist culture. But it does mean that we have to develop a critical relationship to texts, as we learn to bring our own questions framed within the fears, anxieties and hopes of a post-Holocaust world, seek out their inspiration and pass on their wisdom. There is much to learn and much to pass on, but we can only do this if we have learned from the traditions ourselves. We can remember the words of Isaiah . . . 'Cease to do evil and learn to do right. Pursue justice and champion the oppressed, give the orphan their rights and plead the widow's cause' (Isaiah 1:11–17). It is the memory of the journey from slavery in Egypt that is adduced time and time again in Biblical texts to justify the obligation to justice for others: 'For you know the heart of the stranger . . . for you were strangers in the land of Egypt . . .' (Deuteronomy 10:19).

Notes

1. As Anne Karpf concluded in 1996, 'Britain still hasn't managed properly to acknowledge and integrate the trauma of its refugee and survivor communities', *The War After* (p. 245).
2. For some understanding of Jewish experience in contemporary Poland set in historical context, see Eva Hoffman, *Shtetl* (London, Secker & Warburg, 1998).
3. Poland's silence lasted until the publication in 1987 of an article by Jan Blonski 'The Poor Poles Look at the Ghetto' which touched of an extensive and heated debate in Poland about the response to the

extermination of the Jews. It provoked 200 letters and articles. Blonski's article and some of the responses have been translated in Eda Polonsky, *My Brother's Keeper? Recent Polish Debates on the Holocaust* (London, Routledge, 1990)]

4. Ruth Linden has drawn upon post-modern methods in her meetings with survivors to reveal, as I have also been attempting, the intimate connections between an ethnographers lived experience and her interpretations of others. She explores the interconnected processes of remembering, storytelling and self-fashioning in her *Making Stories, Making Selves: Feminist Reflections on the Holocaust* (Columbus, Ohio State University Press, 1993).

5. In different parts of Europe, Jews are learning to come to terms with this anguished inheritance. See for instance, Peter Sichrovsky, *Strangers In Their Own Land: Young Jews in Germany and Austria Today* (London, I.B. Taurus, 1986). In Elena Lappins, *Jewish Voices German Words: Growing up Jewish in Postwar Germany and Austria* (London, Catbird Press, 1994).

6. For some insightful work on the relationship of Judaism to modernity, see, for instance, David Hartman *The Living Covenant* (New York, Free Press, 1985) Norman Lamm Torah Umadda : The Encounter of Religious Learning and Worldly Knowledge in the Jewish Tradition (New York, Ktav, 1990) and Jonathan Sachs, *Tradition in an Untraditional Age* (London, Vallentine Mitchell, 1990) and *The Politics of Hope* (London, Jonathan Cape, 1997).

Appendix

(Notarial Deed)

Before the undersigned Maître René GASTALDI, a Notary Public in Paris, there has appeared:

Mr. Lejzer KRYGER, called Jean MARCZAC, a trader residing in Paris at 5 Rue Massenet, of Polish nationality:

Passport No. 130,826 issued by the Polish Home Office on the thirtieth day of August nineteen hundred and fortynine;

Which said gentleman does not understand the French language and is attended by reason of such fact by Mr. Victor BORTEN, expert translator sworn before the Civil Court of the Seine, residing in Paris at 34 Avenue Hoche;

Who has sworn before the undersigned Notary Public to translate faithfully the statements of the appearing party and the terms of the deed to be set up;

Which appearing party has requested the undersigned Notary to put on record the declarations as made below without proof and this has been allowed to him;

" Having been established in Warsaw before the war as a fur merchant I had both business and friendly relations with the brothers JELENIEWSKI who also were fur merchants in Warsaw;

" I state that the brothers JELENIEWSKI had their business in Warsaw in the Dluga Street. Two of them have perished in the month of April nineteen hundred and fortythree, one having been deported to the Treblinka extermination camp and the other having been killed by the Germans in the Warsaw ghetto. In the course of this same month of March I left the Warsaw ghetto and took refuge in the so-called Aryan part of the city. The third brother JELENIEWSKI with the forename of Chaim I would say in this connection that he was domiciled before the war in Warsaw in the Kaarmalicka Street No. 3, has followed my example and rejoined in that part of the city his wife Guta née Orzel, his children, his sisters-in-law (widows of the two brothers JELENIEWSKI referred to above) and the children of these latter who had been there since the month of March nineteen hundred and fortythree. We were able to find clandestine lodgings in the so-called Aryan part of the City due to the help of a common friend ROMAN CLECHCKI a Catholic Pole. I was accommodated in one flat and Mr. Chaim JELENIEWSKI with the aforesaid members of his family in another one fairly far way.

" Since I got to the so-called Aryan part of Warsaw I have not seen Mr. Chaim JELENIEWSKI again, as the conditions of the time prevented us from leaving our respective refuges. However, we remained in constant touch through the medium of the aforesaid Mr. Roman CIECHOCKI.

" In the month of June nineteen hundred and fortythree I myself on the one hand and the family JELENIEWSKI on the other hand took a decision to take advantage of an opportunity which seemed to offer to leave Poland. The Germans announced at that time that a certain number of Jews would have a possibility of leaving the country by means of payment of substantial sums. The persons desiring to leave were to make a declaration to such effect and were to assemble at the hotel called "Hotel Polski" in Warsaw situate in the Gluga Street where they were to be harboured while awaiting their departure. The Germans promised that these persons could betake themselves to a neutral country.

" I paid on account of the price for departure an instalment of fifty thousand zlotys but, filled with misgivings, I did not go to the said hotel. I have learned from the aforesaid Mr. CIECHOCKI that Mr. Chaim JELENIEWSKI, his wife, his children as also his two sisters-in-law and their children went there round about the tenth of July nineteen hundred and forty-three. It is Mr. CIECHOCKI who made the necessary arrangements for them to proceed to the said hotel and he informed me about it the very same day. Mr. CIECHOCKI who, convinced that the moving over to the hotel Polski was a real chance of salvation, urged me keenly and certainly in good faith to follow their example. I did not follow his counsel and I congratulate myself on this, for indeed the announcement of the possibility of a departure for a neutral country was merely a monstrous trap laid by the Germans. As is at present commonly known, all the people attracted by these deceptive promises who had foregathered at the said hotel were taken to the Warsaw prison called "Pawiak" where they were shot.

" I make this present declaration to affirm solemnly that Mr. Chaim JELENIEWSKI, his wife and his children living clandestinely in Warsaw went in the month of July nineteen hundred and fortythree to the said "Hotel Polski" in the hope of being able thus to leave Poland, which fact can be confirmed if need should be by Mr. Roman CIECHOCKI as aforesaid domiciled at present in Warsaw.

Appendix

And at the same time the appearing party has sworn before the undersigned Notary as to the accuracy of his statements.

FOR DUE RECORD.

Made out and signed in Paris at 13, Avenue Victor Hugo at the office of the undersigned Notary Public;

In the year of NINETEEN HUNDRED AND FIFTY;

On the twentyfirst day of February;

And after due reading of these presents and translation thereof by Mr. BORTEN to Mr. KRYGER, the appearer, these parties have signed together with the Notary.

There follow the signatures and the mention:

Registered in Paris, tenth, notaries on the twentyseventh day of February nineteen hundred and fifty, volume C 924 folio 32, file 1; received five hundred and seventyfive francs (signed) BLANC.

Made out on one sheet
and a half without
amendments or voice
words deleted.
   (signature)   (Endorsement in Hebrew)
                           (Seal of the Legation of
                              Israel).

I, William Smith, Proprietor of the Technical Translation Institute, London, E.C.2. declare that I possess a sound command of the French language and that to my best knowledge and belief the foregoing is a true and faithful translation of the accompanying notarial deed made out by Maître René Gastaldi in Paris on the twentyseventh of February nineteen hundred and fifty.

Declared before me

A Commissioner for Oaths

practising at 34 Coleman Street, London, E.C.2.

Index

Index